What Works:
Research-Based Best Practices in
Developmental Education

Hunter R. Boylan

Continuous Quality Improvement Network
with the

National Center for Developmental Education
Appalachian State University
Boone, NC

ACKNOWLEDGEMENTS

Many people contributed to this work and deserve acknowledgement and a note of thanks for their efforts. Chief among these is Barbara Calderwood who edited this manuscript and, in the process, taught me more than I ever wanted to know about APA style. Thanks also go to my colleague here at the Center, Patrick Saxon, and to Steve Mittelstet, President of Richland College. He and his colleagues were kind enough to review this manuscript and made many useful comments. Finally, I would like to thank my wife, friend, and frequent coauthor, Professor Barbara Bonham, for her patience and support.

Published by the Continuous Quality Improvement Network with the
National Center for Developmental Education
PO Box 32098
Appalachian State University
Boone, NC 28608

Edited by Barbara J. Calderwood

First edition published 2002. Printed in the U.S.A.

ISBN 0-9720147-0-5

Typeset by PreFlight, a Forbes Company
Printed by Forbes Printing
1035 Harper Ave., SW
Lenoir, NC 28645

CONTENTS

INTRODUCTION

Background of Project Partners

This work is the result of collaboration between the Continuous Quality Improvement Network (CQIN) and the National Center for Developmental Education (NCDE). The Continuous Quality Improvement Network (CQIN) is a national association of higher education institutions dedicated to institutional transformation through the application of continuous quality improvement principles. Founded in 1991 by a group of community college presidents, the association seeks "out-of-the-box" solutions to the problems confronted by American 2-year colleges. The Continuous Quality Improvement Network is currently comprised of 35 member institutions including 2- and 4-year nonprofit and corporate partners.

Recognizing that developmental education was a priority for member institutions, CQIN members decided to sponsor a major national study of developmental education. CQIN, therefore, commissioned a national benchmarking study in 1999 to identify and document best practices in the field. It was anticipated that these best practices would include not only general guidelines but also specific practical suggestions for designing the best possible institutional, program, and instructional components of effective developmental education. Furthermore, these best practices would be based on studies of the nation's most effective developmental programs and emphasize actions, services, and concepts that could be applied by any college campus with a serious interest in improving developmental education. The American Productivity and Quality Center (APQC) of Houston, Texas, was, therefore, commissioned to undertake the study as a partner of CQIN and its participating institutions and corporate members.

The American Productivity and Quality Center is a nonprofit organization providing information, training, research, decision support, and networking for organizational performance improvement. The Center specializes in completing benchmarking research. In fact, the Center has won several awards for its work and is generally regarded as one of the outstanding benchmarking research organizations in the United States.

Dr. Hunter R. Boylan, Director of the National Center for Developmental Education and Professor of Higher Education at

Appalachian State University, was selected to serve as the subject matter expert for this study. His role was to assist in designing instruments, analyzing data, identifying best practice institutions, participating in site visits, and verifying the findings of this study.

The National Center for Developmental Education (NCDE), housed at Appalachian State University, is the nation's leading source of research, training, and resources for practitioners in the field of developmental education. The NCDE was founded in 1976 under a grant from the W.K. Kellogg Foundation of Battle Creek, Michigan. The Center publishes the *Journal of Developmental Education*, *Research in Developmental Education*, and occasional technical reports. It also sponsors the Kellogg Institute for the Training and Certification of Developmental Educators; coordinates Appalachian State University's graduate programs in developmental education; provides resource information to institutions and developmental education professionals; delivers technical services to colleges, universities, and educational agencies; and conducts contract and other research studies.

The NCDE had previously conducted several major studies of developmental education. These included:

- the National Study of Developmental Education carried out from 1989 through 1996 under a grant from the Exxon Education Foundation,
- the study of minority retention in developmental education undertaken from 1995-1997 under a grant from the Alfred P. Sloan Foundation,
- two statewide studies of the Texas Academic Skills Program and developmental education in Texas colleges and universities carried out in 1995-96 and 1998 under a grant from the Texas Higher Education Coordinating Board,
- a series of literature reviews on best practices in developmental education carried out in 1998-99 under a grant from the League for Innovation, and
- a variety of other research studies conducted under contract to state and federal higher education agencies.

It was agreed that the NCDE would combine relevant findings from its research with results from the CQIN/APQC benchmarking study to produce a single volume describing research-based best practices in the field of developmental education.

The goal of this project was to provide policy makers, administrators, and practitioners with a guide for program design, development, and improvement based on the best of current research in the field of developmental education. The Continuous Quality Improvement Network and the National Center for Developmental Education join in expressing their hope that readers will use the information in this volume to improve the quality of practice in contemporary developmental education.

Definitions

For the purposes of this study developmental education is defined as courses or services provided for the purpose of helping underprepared college students attain their academic goals. The term underprepared students refers to any students who need to develop their cognitive or affective abilities in order to succeed in a postsecondary educational experience.

Underprepared students exhibit a broad range of talents and levels. As the motto of the National Association for Developmental Education defines it, developmental education helps "underprepared students prepare, prepared students advance, and advanced students excel." Many programs in this study provide services ranging from remedial instruction in reading to graduate and professional school test preparation.

As used in this study, the term developmental program is defined as any organized collection of courses and/or services designed to help underprepared students succeed. The programs in this study all have provided some combination of courses and support services to their students.

Best practices refer to organizational, administrative, instructional, counseling, advising, and tutoring activities engaged in by highly successful developmental programs. These practices are typically validated by the research and the literature in developmental education.

Methodology of the CQIN/APQC Study

The CQIN/APQC study was initiated in the Fall of 1999 and continued through the Summer of 2000. It represented the largest and most extensive benchmarking study ever undertaken in the field of developmental education. Twelve colleges and one corporate partner provided funding for the study and formed the CQIN/APQC study team which assisted in reviewing findings and participated in site visits.

The study involved two phases. In the first phase "best practice" institutions were identified through primary and secondary research as well as nominations from sponsoring organizations. Initially, nearly 60 institutions were considered for inclusion in the study because they had strong reputations for delivering developmental education successfully. Of these, 36 institutions agreed to participate in, complete surveys, and provide data for the study.

A series of extensive survey instruments were developed, field tested, and reviewed by project personnel. Instrumentation was based on models that had been previously found to be successful by APQC but adapted for studying college and university developmental education. These instruments were then used to gather information from participating institutions. Survey data was reviewed by APQC staff and Dr. Boylan to identify institutions with the strongest developmental programs based on the criteria of:

- developmental education program strategy,
- instructional functions for developmental education,
- learner support functions, and
- evaluation methods and outcomes.

Using these criteria, the list of best-practice institutions was narrowed through several rounds of analysis and review. In each round, APQC project staff, CQIN sponsoring institutions, and NCDE staff reviewed data and identified programs whose services and outcomes were highly effective and represented the best of current practice.

Eventually five institutions, four community colleges and one university, were selected as exemplars of best practices in developmental education. These institutions were Durham Technical College in Raleigh, North Carolina, the General College of the University of Minnesota in Minneapolis, Minnesota, Hudson Valley Community College in Troy, New York, Oakton Community College in Des Plaines, Illinois, and Richland College in Dallas, Texas.

In the second phase of the project the CQIN/APQC study team developed a site visit question and discussion guide to gather further data from best-practice institutions. Each of these institutions was visited by members of the CQIN/APQC study team and accompanied by faculty and staff from sponsoring colleges. During the site visits, key personnel were asked questions based on the site visit discussion guide. The study team developed transcripts of site visit discussions and then collated and analyzed this information to develop extensive case study reports for each of the best-practice institutions.

The initial dissemination of study findings was limited to the original group of sponsoring institutions who were represented at a knowledge transfer conference held at APQC headquarters in Houston, Texas, in August of 2000. Recognizing that this information could be of great value to the field, however, CQIN invited the National Center for Developmental Education to join them in producing a guide to best practices in developmental education.

How to Use this Guide

Each section of this book addresses a particular aspect of developmental education. Each section includes a description of specific best practices as well as a summary of research supporting the efficacy of the practice. For each best practice a specific institutional example of its application is provided. Examples for best-practice applications were drawn from the CQIN/APQC (2000) benchmarking study as well from the literature and from observations of NCDE staff.

Finally, each best practice is followed by a list of tips for implementation of best practices. Although the best practices cited are well grounded in research, tips for implementation are based on the observations and experiences of the author and the staff of the National Center for Developmental Education. The tips provided are not necessarily research based. Instead they are based on experience and observation of successful developmental education activities.

An inventory of research-based best practices is provided in the last section of this book. Readers are encouraged to use this inventory to compare their institution's developmental education efforts to those of best-practice institutions and to the research on developmental education. This will enable them to determine where their institution fits along a continuum of best-practice applications in developmental education.

It is recommended that the best-practice inventory be completed by groups of at least five individuals involved in developmental education and that ratings of an institution's compliance with best-practice standards be determined by consensus of these individuals. This permits a more balanced approach to assessment of developmental education on an individual campus.

There are probably many organizational, administrative, service, and instructional delivery innovations in developmental education that are not cited in this study. This is because they did not meet the criteria established for inclusion. In order to be cited as a "best practice," a condition or activity had to meet the following criteria:

(a) it must have been cited in several scientific research studies of effective developmental education,

(b) it must have been cited over time in the research on effective developmental education,

(c) it must have been successfully replicated at several college or university campuses,

(d) it must have been considered by expert professionals participating in the study as important for developmental education, and

(e) it must have had supporting research and evaluation data using sound methodology to validate its effectiveness at institutions where it has been applied.

There is a great variety of sound approaches to providing developmental education. Many of those not cited here can contribute to successful developmental education. Even if they have not been the subject of substantial research they may produce positive results for developmental education programs and students. However, if they did not meet the outlined criteria, they were not included in this report.

There are many people who will read about the best practices cited here and say, "we can't do that at our institution." To this, we can only respond that there are more than 25 years of research to validate what works in developmental education. We can only ask, why are you doing something else?

CHAPTER 1

Organizational, Administrative, and Institutional Practices

As Noel, Levitz, and Saluri (1985) point out, retention is an institutional, not a program responsibility. The same is true with developmental education. Developmental education does not work well when an institution's chief academic officers try to pretend that it does not exist. Developmental education does not work well when it is consigned to the periphery of institutional endeavors. Developmental education does not work well when it is a random, nonsystematic effort carried out by uncoordinated units spread across the institutional flow chart. Developmental education does not work well when faculty complain that "these students don't belong here." Developmental education does not work well when academic advisors tell students that they should try to avoid taking non-credit developmental courses and get on with the regular curriculum.

If developmental education is to be successful, it must be an institutional priority supported by the institutional community. It must be coordinated, and it must be part of institutional planning efforts. If these conditions are not met, then whatever activities are undertaken in support of developmental education will not reach their full potential. If these conditions are not met, then, in spite of whatever valiant efforts may be carried out by a handful of individuals, developmental students may still fail to fully profit from the developmental education experience.

The actions described in this chapter establish the conditions under which developmental education can operate most successfully. Without institutional support, coordination, integration, and collaboration, campus developmental education activities cannot produce the benefits these activities were designed to attain.

1.1: Centralization of Program Activities

Centralized developmental programs have consistently been found to be more successful than decentralized developmental programs (Donovan, 1974; Boylan, Bliss, & Bonham, 1997; Roueche & Baker, 1987; Roueche

& Snow, 1977). Centralization refers to an organizational arrangement in which developmental courses and services are highly coordinated, housed in a single department or program, and headed by a chair or director. Decentralization refers to those programs for which there is little or no coordination of the developmental education effort, there are developmental courses and services offered in different departments and programs, and there is no campus-wide administrator for developmental education.

The National Study of Developmental Education (Boylan, Bliss, & Bonham, 1997) reported that, as of the mid-1990s, 52% of all the nation's developmental education programs were centralized. An earlier report from this study (Boylan, Bonham, Claxton, & Bliss, 1992) suggested that centralized programs were somewhat less common in community colleges than in universities. This was also supported by a survey conducted by the American Association of Community Colleges (Shults, 2000) indicating that in community colleges, 61% of developmental education courses were decentralized. In spite of decades of research recommending the opposite approach, the majority of community colleges appeared to adopt a decentralized approach to developmental education.

There is, of course, a continuum of centralization. At the low end, some developmental courses, usually English, reading, and mathematics, are grouped together as a single department. These courses are, as a minimum, closely coordinated with laboratories or learning centers. At the high end, all developmental courses including study skills, freshmen seminars, critical thinking courses, and the like are combined with academic support services, learning laboratories, or learning assistance centers and organized as a single department or program. Frequently in centralized programs developmental students have their own academic advisors. Fully centralized programs, therefore, are characterized by:

- having several developmental subject areas (usually reading, writing, and mathematics) coordinated under a single unit,
- having an overarching and clearly articulated philosophy of developmental education to guide program efforts,
- combining support services and laboratories within this unit, and
- having a single individual responsible for coordinating the campus wide developmental education effort, usually a coordinator or a director.

Research suggests that any variation of centralization appears to result in stronger program performance than completely decentralized organizational arrangements (Boylan & Saxon, 1998). The more centralized a program is, however, the greater its likelihood of success. This is particularly true when there is strong institutional support for the mission of developmental education (Kiemig, 1983; Roueche & Roueche, 1999).

In several studies of exemplary developmental programs, John Roueche and his colleagues consistently found that centralization of program efforts was related to student success (Roueche & Baker, 1987; Roueche & Roueche, 1999; Roueche & Snow, 1977). In a study of Texas developmental education, Boylan and Saxon (1998) found that centralized programs produced higher postdevelopmental education pass rates on a state mandated test than decentralized programs. Results from the National Study of Developmental Education (Boylan, Bliss, & Bonham, 1997) indicated that centralized program structure was related to improved student retention and higher pass rates in developmental education. A study sponsored by the Continuous Quality Improvement Network/American Productivity and Quality Center (CQIN/APQC, 2000) found that, among best-practice institutions, "successful developmental education programs are structured as academic departments within their institutions" (p.42). Overwhelmingly research results provided evidence that the best organizational arrangement for developmental education included a centralized program combining a variety of courses and services.

———〜〜〜———

A good example of a centralized developmental program is found at Guilford Technical and Community College in Jamestown, North Carolina. In this program, developmental reading, study skills, English, mathematics, and college success courses along with the learning laboratory and tutoring programs are combined as a single program and headed by a Director of Developmental Education. The director serves as the campus-wide coordinator of developmental education as well as the program's liaison to campus administrators, the community, and other academic units. Two assistant directors coordinate faculty and provide orientation and training for adjunct instructors teaching developmental courses.

———〜〜〜———

Tips on Centralization

- Always bear in mind that the primary benefits of centralization are coordination of the developmental education effort and enhanced communication among those involved in this effort. Unless a centralized program is highly coordinated and the people working in it communicate regularly, the benefits of centralization will be lost.
- The fewer the layers of bureaucracy between the developmental program director and the chief academic officer of the institution, the more likely it is that the program will be integrated into the institutional mainstream.
- A centralized program is best coordinated by a full-time administrator. The fewer extra responsibilities the administrator has, the more likely he or she is to exploit the benefits of centralization. This is particularly true for large developmental programs serving 1,000 students or more.
- Centralized developmental programs have many names. In community colleges they are most frequently called "Department of Developmental Education," "Center for Academic Development," "Learning Assistance Program," or "Academic Advancement Department." What the program is called, however, is far less important to its success than the extent to which its activities are integrated into the institution. The National Study of Developmental Education (Boylan, Bonham, Claxton, & Bliss, 1992) found no relationship between what a program was called and how well its students performed.
- Large centralized developmental programs frequently have lead instructors or coordinators for each subject area being taught. A major function of these lead instructors or coordinators is to promote coordination and communication among those teaching in that subject area. However, it is also important that these coordinators insure that there is coordination and communication across the disciplines being taught in the program.
- The value of centralization is not limited to courses alone. Many centralized programs also include learning laboratories and centers, tutoring programs, and other support services as part of the developmental education unit.

1.2: Coordination of Developmental Education Courses and Services

Although a centralized developmental program may be desirable, local campus traditions, politics, or economics may often prohibit the establishment of a centralized program. Even if developmental courses and services are provided through a decentralized organizational structure, however, they can still be coordinated. In fact, it appears that a highly coordinated although decentralized developmental education organizational structure may be nearly as effective as a centralized structure in some ways.

The CQIN/APQC (2000) study found that although the overwhelming majority of exemplary programs were centralized, those that were decentralized featured a high level of integration and communication among courses and services. These decentralized exemplary programs also had an administrator who was either officially or unofficially responsible for the campus-wide coordination of developmental education activities.

In their analysis of data from the National Study of Developmental Education, Boylan, Bliss, and Bonham (1997) found that some decentralized programs produced outcomes comparable to centralized programs. The difference, however, was in the level of coordination. Those decentralized developmental programs with a high degree of coordination had student success rates in developmental courses closely comparable to those of decentralized programs. Decentralized programs without coordination were usually inferior in all measures of student success (Boylan & Saxon, 1998).

Decentralized but highly coordinated programs are characterized by:

- regular meetings of all those involved in the delivery of developmental courses and services,
- articulation of common goals and objectives for all developmental courses and services,
- integration of developmental courses and academic support services, and
- coordination of developmental courses and services by an administrator with primary responsibility for campus-wide developmental education.

If developmental programs are not centralized, it is important that some method be used to insure that those teaching developmental courses and providing academic support services interact with each other on a regular basis. According to the CQIN/APQC study (2000), for instance, in successful developmental programs, "developmental education faculty routinely share instructional strategies" (p. 34).

It is also important that this interaction among faculty and staff be based on an understanding of the mission of developmental education and a common set of goals for developmental students. This is why coordination of the developmental education effort is required. Otherwise, well meaning faculty and staff may end up working at cross purposes or needlessly duplicating efforts. Worse still, they may fail to see emerging patterns of student or program performance that need to be either corrected or reinforced.

According to the American Association for Higher Education (1992), learning is "multidimensional, integrated, and revealed over time" (p. 2). The multidimensional and integrated aspects of student learning are unlikely to be noticed, let alone acted upon, by individuals who fail to communicate with each other in a systematic manner.

If centralization is not possible, then full-time instructors teaching developmental courses in any subject area can at least meet as a group a minimum of twice a semester to monitor student performance, discuss problems, seek solutions, and share experiences. Adjunct instructors teaching developmental courses should either be invited to attend these meetings or provided with opportunities to meet separately. Staff members who provide academic support services for developmental students should also participate as equal partners in these meetings.

In addition, all those involved in the developmental education effort should meet to identify common goals for that effort. These should then be communicated to all those involved in developmental education, including students. Furthermore, developmental education activities should be integrated to the extent that they are mutually supportive. The activities of tutors, learning laboratory staff, and advisors should support the activities of developmental instructors.

For these things to happen, some campus administrator must be responsible for coordinating them. This is why campuses with effective decentralized developmental education activities usually have an administrator with primary responsibility for developmental education on a campus-wide basis.

—〰—

Austin Community College has a decentralized program in which developmental courses are taught in individual academic departments. However, developmental faculty on each campus meet regularly to discuss what is going on in their courses and to share ideas and teaching techniques. Furthermore, the Assistant Vice President of Austin Community College has major responsibility for the system-wide coordination of developmental education. In essence, she provides centralization and coordination for the developmental education effort. To support this, coordination committees have been established on each campus to monitor developmental education efforts.

—〰—

Tips on Coordination

- Coordination of the developmental education effort requires face-to-face meeting time for those involved in that effort. Developmental education personnel should meet at least once a month to discuss program problems, seek solutions, monitor outcomes, and plan for the future.
- Meetings of developmental educators provide an opportunity to encourage professional development. Occasionally, meetings of developmental educators should be focused on the discussion of relevant books or articles in the field.
- Everyone directly involved in developmental education activities should participate in at least three meetings during an academic term. This includes faculty and staff. It is essential that instructors, counselors, tutors, and learning specialists all be part of a coordinated developmental education effort.
- Institutional personnel whose activities support developmental education should periodically be invited to meetings of campus developmental educators so that they will know what is going on in developmental education and be better able to support it. Examples of those who should be involved in such meetings are registrars,

admissions officers, institutional research officers, advising coordinators, and vocational/technical coordinators.

- A campus wide advisory committee for the developmental program is often useful. This committee should include, among others, representatives from the academic departments in which developmental students will enroll following completion of developmental courses.

1.3: Management of Faculty and Student Expectations of Developmental Education

The CQIN/APQC (2000) study has found that "Successful developmental education programs effectively manage both faculty members' and students' expectations regarding developmental education" (p. 12). Best-practice institutions go to substantial lengths to make sure that everyone understands what developmental education can and cannot do at any given campus. They also go to similar lengths to make sure that faculty, staff, and students know what is expected of them to support the developmental education effort. In best-practice institutions, advisors, instructors, administrators, and support services personnel know that each group has an important role to play in making developmental education successful.

Successful developmental programs make the goals and objectives of developmental education explicit and take actions to insure that both students and faculty understand these goals and objectives. These programs have clear definitions of student success in developmental education and these, too, are made explicit to faculty and students. Furthermore, the campus community at best-practice institutions is regularly advised of the extent to which developmental education is successful in accomplishing its stated goals and objectives.

Expectations are also managed by insuring that faculty teaching developmental courses, both full-time and adjunct, were hired specifically for the job. Hiring committees seek faculty with specific training and/or experience in developmental instruction. Those hired are oriented to the expectations of developmental education before undertaking their duties. They are also provided with in-service training to assist them in meeting these expectations. In addition, they are expected to participate in local and national developmental education professional organizations.

The management of expectations as a characteristic of successful developmental programs has been well-documented in the literature (Casazza & Silverman, 1996; Kiemig, 1983; Roueche & Roueche,1993; Roueche & Roueche, 1999). Although the CQIN/APQC (2000) study was not the first to discover this finding, it is the most recent study to reaffirm the importance of insuring that everyone knows what is expected of developmental faculty, staff, and students.

——∿∿∿——

Richland College hires faculty specifically to teach developmental courses. Candidates for full-time teaching positions are required to conduct a teaching demonstration as part of the interview and hiring process. Hiring teams including developmental educators screen out individuals who fail to demonstrate the attitudes and instructional practices that contribute to the success of developmental students. In addition, those who teach developmental courses are required to participate in orientation and professional development activities relevant to developmental instruction.

——∿∿∿——

Tips on Management of Expectations

- Those hired to teach developmental courses should undergo detailed orientation to the mission, goals, objectives, and expectations of developmental education. Individuals who disagree with these goals, objectives, or expectations should be assigned to other teaching duties. This should be true for full-time and part-time instructors assigned to developmental courses.
- A key to managing expectations of developmental education is defining "successful developmental education." Success in developmental education should not be measured solely through student grades in courses. Other measures of student development may also be incorporated into the definition of success. Once a definition is agreed upon, it should be widely disseminated to the campus community.
- Management of expectations of developmental education requires that the activities of developmental education be communicated to all components of the institutional community. This may be done

through newsletters, email messages, dissemination of program reports, or departmental briefings.

- It is not only the responsibility of developmental educators to manage expectations. The entire campus community should collaborate in stipulating the definition of success in developmental education and making explicit the purpose and anticipated outcomes of developmental education.

- It is particularly important for adjunct and part-time faculty to be part of the process of managing expectations of developmental education. These faculty members are often responsible for teaching a substantial share of developmental courses. Expectations of developmental students and faculty should be clearly defined as part of the orientation of adjunct and part-time faculty.

- Expectations for developmental education should be clearly specified in any manuals or other documents provided for the purpose of orienting adjunct and part-time faculty.

1.4: Collaboration with Other Academic Units

Norton Grubb and his colleagues (1999) found that "remediation is usually organized as an activity separate from the core purposes, isolated in jigsaw puzzle of... programs" (p. 172). In essence, developmental education and its practitioners were segregated from the institutional mainstream and had little contact with other academic professionals. This characterization appeared to be true at most of the community colleges studied by Grubb. However, this was not true of those identified as best-practice institutions by the CQIN/APQC (2000) study.

All the best-practice programs in this study engaged in collaborative activities with other campus academic units. Rather than being isolated from the institutional mainstream, the programs and their staff were actively involved in consulting, collaborating, and problem solving with other departments and academic units. They were aggressive in seeking ways of sharing their expertise across the campus and in establishing working relationships with other segments of the campus community.

As a result, at best-practice institutions, developmental educators were seen not only as expert professionals but also as equal partners in pursuit of the college's academic mission. Research over the past 20 years has validated intrainstitutional collaboration as an important component of successful developmental programs. Kiemig (1983) found that such collaboration was a key feature in developing campus-wide support for developmental education goals and objectives. Maxwell (1997) and Stratton (1998) argued that developmental educators have knowledge and skills that may be helpful to other faculty members who wish to improve their instructional delivery and classroom environments. Roueche and Roueche (1999) pointed out that the most successful developmental programs went to great lengths to collaborate with other campus units in order to promote learning from one another.

For a variety of reasons, it is important for developmental educators to participate as active members of the local academic community. This includes working with other academic units to solve common problems. It involves serving as consultants and sharing expertise with other campus units. It involves serving on institutional governing bodies or working as members of college-wide task forces and committees. These activities enable developmental educators to be perceived as professional partners in academe and enhances their credibility and professional image. It also enables them to share their professional expertise with others and to learn from other professionals at their institution.

———\~\~\~———

Developmental educators at Hudson Valley Community College are engaged in a variety of collaborative activities with their colleagues. Developmental education faculty and learning assistance personnel provide workshops on how to work with "at-risk" students during faculty development days. Learning center personnel have conducted workshops for the mathematics department on interactive computer algebra systems. Learning center personnel have also provided in-class workshops on study skills in a variety of nondevelopmental courses.

———\~\~\~———

Tips on Collaboration

- Developmental education faculty and staff should be encouraged to participate in the governance of the institution. They should sit on college governance bodies, serve on campus committees, and participate in college task forces. This helps to establish their credentials as members of the campus community and promotes collaboration with other campus units.

- Collaborative relationships have to be built over time. Initial collaborative ventures between developmental educators and other campus units should "start small"; have a specific, measurable focus; and specify a clear end point.

- Collaboration works best when it addresses issues that all parties recognize as important and necessary to the health and well being of the organization. The extent to which any individual collaborative activity is perceived as important by the campus community is of greater value than the number of collaborative activities.The parties involved should clearly establish the criteria by which the success of any collaborative venture will be judged at the outset of that venture. This will reduce the possibility of confusion or debate at some later date over whether or not the project has been successful.

- Those involved in collaboration should bear in mind that its purpose is not for developmental educators to tell others what they know. True collaboration is not one-sided but involves learning from each other.

- Collaboration should not be limited to the local institution or community. Collaboration may also involve working with other colleges or universities on projects of mutual interest. Developmental educators, for instance, might share data with other developmental programs in their state to identify baseline performance trends. They might sponsor cooperative site visits with other developmental programs in their state or region. They might engage in collaborative projects with "feeder" high schools or, in the case of community colleges, with the universities in which their students typical enroll after completing transfer requirements.

- Developmental educators might also collaborate with other campus professionals in writing articles or developing presentations for conferences. This not only provides opportunities to share ideas, it also demonstrates the professionalism of developmental educators.

1.5: Establishment of Clearly Defined Mission, Goals, and Objectives

More than a quarter of a century ago, one of the first national studies of developmental education found that successful programs were characterized by the presence of a clearly defined mission statement supported by written goals and objectives (Donovan, 1974). This finding was consistently reaffirmed in studies by Cross (1976), Roueche and Snow (1977), Roueche and Baker (1987), Boylan, Bonham, Claxton, and Bliss (1992), and McCabe (2000).

The National Study of Developmental Education (Boylan, Bonham, Claxton, & Bliss, 1992) found that developmental programs with written statements of mission, goals, and objectives had higher student pass rates in developmental courses than programs without such statements. In a study of Texas developmental education, Boylan and Saxon (1998) found that developmental programs with written statements of mission, goals, and objectives had higher postdevelopmental education pass rates on a state mandated test. They also had higher year-to-year retention rates for developmental students than programs without written statements of goals and objectives.

As Casazza and Silverman (1996) point out, "Successful programs begin with a well-defined mission statement and a set of program goals addressing specific areas" (p. 72). A written statement of mission, goals, and objectives usually includes the following components:

- a brief statement of the mission of developmental education on a particular campus,
- a general statement of the overall goals that developmental education is expected to attain, and
- a longer listing of the specific objectives that are to be accomplished in order to attain goals.

A typical mission statement might be "To insure that students have every opportunity to be successful in college." A typical goal statement might be "To provide students with the basic academic skills required for mastery of the college curriculum." A typical objective statement might be that "Students will be able to use the World Wide Web to conduct research for class assignments." As these examples show, a mission statement identifies the broadest purpose of developmental education. Goal statements break this mission statement down into general expectations of the developmental program. Statements of objectives identify the specific activities that will be undertaken or skills that will be taught in order to accomplish these goals.

The statement of mission, goals, and objectives should be developed collaboratively among all those involved in the developmental effort. This includes faculty teaching developmental courses as well as those teaching regular curriculum courses, staff providing support services, and appropriate academic and student affairs administrators.

Furthermore, the statement of mission, goals, and objectives is not a static document. It should be reviewed annually and modified periodically. It should also be widely shared with all those involved in the developmental education effort. This not only includes program faculty and staff; it also includes students.

As Cross has noted (1976), developmental students are likely to perform better in programs in which expectations are made clear through the specification of goals and objectives. Explaining the program's mission, goals, and objectives, therefore, should be an important part of orienting students to a developmental education program. It should also be a key component of orientation for new faculty and staff.

———∽∞∽———

Southeastern Community College in Whiteville, North Carolina has developed a statement called "The Message" which appears in the syllabi of developmental courses and which all faculty share and discuss with first-year students. "The Message" emphasizes students' responsibility for their own learning and is based on the goals of developmental education as well as developmental instructors' expectations of students. The text of the message is...

As a student, you have basic responsibility for your success: our responsibility is to assist you in meeting your educational goals. The message below will help you take responsibility for your own academic success.

Set goals and evaluate them.

Ask, "Why am I here? What do I want to do? Where do I see myself in two years? What are my long-term goals." Have a clear understanding of where you are. Have a reasonable plan involving realistic goals and a realistic time frame.

Know what it takes to be successful.

This is what it takes to be successful. Do them consistently!

❐ Attend class regularly.
❐ Complete all assignments by the due date.
❐ Participate fully in class.
❐ Schedule regular outside study time.
❐ Use college survival skills information.
❐ Participate in college life outside class.
❐ Request help when needed.

Know where to find help.

❐ Your instructor
❐ Your advisor
❐ Counseling office
❐ A peer advisor
❐ Class study groups

Adapted from Southeastern Community College, Whiteville, NC, 1998.

—〰—

Tips on Goals and Objectives

- A mission statement should consist of one or two sentences stating the primary purpose of the program. For instance, "The mission of the developmental education program is to prepare students for success in their chosen program of study."

- Statements of goals describe an end result the program hopes to accomplish. Statements of objectives describe what activities will take place to accomplish these goals. Both should be kept simple in order to promote clarity.

- Goal statements, in general, are more specific than mission statements. Statements of objectives are more specific than statements of goals.

- Goal statements can often be used to evaluate the outcomes of a program. For instance, if a goal of the program is to "prepare students to be successful in college level English courses," then the percentage of students who complete the program and pass their college-level English courses is a valid measure of the program's impact.

- The program's goals and objectives can often be improved if students who have completed developmental education review them to determine if they are appropriate. Although students may not be well equipped to determine program goals and objectives, they are perhaps better equipped than anyone else to determine if these goals and objectives have been realized in their own experience with developmental education.

- The program's mission, goals, and objectives should be shared widely. This helps inform the campus community of the role of developmental education.

- The National Association for Developmental Education has published a self-evaluation guide for developmental programs (Thayer, 1995). This guide can be quite useful in developing a program's mission, goals, and objectives.

1.6: Identification of Developmental Education as an Institutional Priority

It should come as no surprise that developmental education is most successful at institutions that consider it to be a priority. In the CQIN/APQC study (2000), a survey of 28 exemplary developmental programs revealed that all but one of them rated developmental education as "completely" or "extensively" important as an institutional priority. In their study of developmental education in Texas colleges and universities, Boylan and Saxon (1998) found that programs with the highest student retention rates were housed in institutions that considered developmental education to be a priority. Several studies conducted by John Roueche and his colleagues at The University of Texas indicated that the most successful developmental programs were hosted by institutions that considered the developmental education effort to be a key component of the institutional mission (Roueche & Baker, 1987; Roueche & Roueche, 1993; Roueche & Roueche, 1999).

When developmental education is considered an institutional priority, several things are present (CQIN/APQC, 2000).

- There is consistency between institutional goals and the goals of developmental education.
- Developmental education is mentioned prominently in institutional publications, particularly the college catalog.
- Developmental education is part of the institution's long range planning.
- Faculty, administrators, and staff share a common vision of what developmental education is seeking to accomplish.
- Members of the campus community outside of developmental education consider it to be important even if they are not involved in it.

Although it is important to identify developmental education as an institutional priority, it should also be considered an institution-wide responsibility. In work that is now regarded as a classic in the field, Ruth Kiemig (1983) has reported that developmental education is most effective when it is regarded as a responsibility of the entire institution rather than a responsibility of a single program or a collection of services. In such a situation all campus administrative, academic, and student services share the goal of developing students' personal and academic skills.

This sentiment is echoed by Noel and Levitz (1985) who point out that the retention of students is not the sole responsibility of a single campus unit but, rather, an institution-wide responsibility. All students are more likely to succeed when the resources of the institution are marshaled and organized in such a way as to provide support for student development.

Unfortunately, even though the importance of making developmental education an institutional priority is clearly documented in the literature, relatively few community colleges have actually done so. In preparing this book, NCDE staff reviewed a random sample of 50 community college catalogs and 25 university catalogs. They found that developmental education was listed as part of the institutional mission statement in only 9 community college catalogs. None of the university catalogs reviewed listed developmental education as part of the institutional mission statement.

Making developmental education an institutional priority is difficult given the many purposes and responsibilities of the modern community college. Nevertheless, it is possible to do if institutional leaders are committed to it. Such a commitment must come from the top down as well as the bottom up.

Discussions among various faculty groups, student affairs personnel, and institutional administrators must take place to identify how each of these constituencies can support a commitment to developmental education. Institutional leaders, however, must take the initiative in articulating the importance of developmental education to the campus community.

———∾∾∾———

Pima County Communty College in Tucson, Arizona, has established developmental education as a system-wide priority. The chancellor of the system regularly reinforces the institution's commitment to developmental education in public statements. Campus presidents and deans of instruction are held accountable for including developmental education in institutional planning. A system-wide task force of developmental educators, academic support personnel, and administrators meets regularly to identify indicators of commitment to developmental education and to monitor campus implementation of these indicators.

———∾∾∾———

Tips on Making Developmental Education an Institutional Priority

- Developmental education is more likely to be seen as an institutional priority if its goals and objectives are consistent with the institutional mission. Periodic reviews of developmental education goals and objectives should be undertaken to insure that they continue to be consistent with the institutional mission.

- Key institutional administrators should review the goals and objectives of the developmental education program to make sure that it is doing what it was designed to do as well as what administrators want it to do.

- Administrators are more likely to support developmental education if they are provided with evaluation results demonstrating that the program is successful in accomplishing goals and objectives consistent with the institutional mission.

- The campus community in general and administrators in particular must know of the activities, successes, needs, and problems of developmental education if they are to support it. Newsletters, email announcements, evaluation results, and program reports should be shared widely with those in a position to support developmental education.

- A campus-wide advisory board representing a cross-section of the campus community is a valuable tool in establishing developmental education as a priority. If other members of the campus community have input into program operations and are briefed on program activities, they are in a better position to support developmental education and value its contributions.

- Developmental students frequently represent a substantial percentage of the graduates of a given institution. Although no formal studies are found in the literature, many colleges and universities report informally that anywhere from 10% to 50% of their graduates were once enrolled in developmental education. This can be a useful statistic in eliciting institutional support for developmental education.

- Institutional support is more likely to be forthcoming if developmental education professionals are active participants in campus committees, advisory boards, or governing bodies. Such participation helps to enhance the perception that developmental educators are part of the campus community.

1.7: Provision of Comprehensive Support Services

In their meta-analysis of the literature on developmental education, Kulik, Kulik, and Schwalb (1983) found that the provision of comprehensive support services characterized programs with high rates of student retention. Roueche and Roueche (1993, 1999) reported similar findings in their ongoing research on effective community college programs for developmental students. Boylan and Saxon (1998) found that the more comprehensive the services available to underprepared students, the more likely those students were to pass the state-mandated TASP test in Texas.

The message of these findings is that institutions that provide only remedial courses in response to the presence of underprepared students are unlikely to have great success in serving these students. Providing remedial courses is probably the most efficient and cost-effective way of serving underprepared students. It is easiest to "batch process" developmental students by assessing their academic needs and then putting them into courses designed to meet these needs. Larger numbers of students may therefore be accommodated using what is, essentially, an assembly line model. Furthermore, the use of courses to respond to student underpreparedness generates FTEs and subsequent revenue for the college. Support services, on the other hand, are more labor intensive and rarely generate revenue directly. Nevertheless, colleges cannot expect to attain high rates of student success and retention unless they provide a diversified range of academic and personal support services.

Although most community colleges provide a variety of support services, these services are often distributed throughout the institution in different departments and programs. A study of Texas developmental education (Boylan et al., 1996) reported that, in the majority of institutions, personnel providing these services rarely interact with each other and support services are seldom highly coordinated. As a result, an institution may provide a comprehensive array of support services but developmental students' access to them is random.

Comprehensive developmental education services must be provided to developmental students on a systematic rather than a random basis (Boylan et al., 1996). A systematic approach to the provision of comprehensive support services requires provision of the following services in a coordinated manner:

- student skills' assessment,
- academic advising,
- study strategies courses or workshops,
- group and individual tutoring,
- individualized instruction often supported by computers, and
- learning assistance centers and/or learning laboratories.

This list might be looked upon as a basic menu of academic and support services. Many institutions also provide other services to developmental students such as first-year experience programs, freshmen seminars, mentoring programs, critical thinking courses, learning communities, and personal counseling. All of these have been shown to contribute to the success of both developmental and nondevelopmental students (Neuburger, 1999).

Developmental students are usually a very diverse group. The greater the variety of services available to them, the greater the likelihood not only that students will use these services but also that one or more of the services will offer the support necessary for their particular learning preferences.

Hudson Valley Community College in Troy, New York has an extensive academic support system featuring group and individual tutoring, short- and long-term workshops on a variety of topics related to student success, learning laboratories, and academic advising. This program features such components as in-class workshops on study strategies, tutoring open houses, and academic counseling by trained faculty. Learning center staff at Hudson Valley Community College also conduct in-class study skills, time management, and other workshops at the request of faculty in basic skills and content areas.

Tips on Comprehensive Support Services

- It is often helpful to take an inventory of all campus services that may be relevant to developmental education and develop a listing of these services for referrals by developmental education faculty and staff. Many services, such as day care, personal counseling, or job placement, may be of value to developmental students.

- Campus services are not the only source of support available to developmental students. Off-campus community, religious, and social service agencies should also be considered as a valuable source of support to developmental students.

- It is advisable that, just as the goals and objectives of the developmental program should be consistent with the institutional mission, the goals and objectives of developmental education component services should be consistent with the overall goals and objectives of the developmental program.

- It is important that college academic advisors be well-briefed on the nature and purpose of various academic support services so that they can appropriately refer students to these services as part of the academic advising process. Advisors must "buy in" to the importance of developmental education if they are to wholeheartedly support student participation in it and counsel students accordingly.

- It is essential that all courses and support services connected with developmental education be viewed as a system rather than as random activities. Developmental educators should make consistent efforts to insure that courses and support services are well integrated with one another. Students should also be encouraged to conceive of and to take advantage of developmental courses and services on a systematic basis.

- Students are more likely to take advantage of and profit from support services if they are located in close proximity to classrooms (Boylan, Bonham, Claxton, & Bliss, 1992). Although the physical facilities of courses and services are difficult to move, the need for them to be in proximity to each other should be taken into account as new facilities are built or renovated.

1.8: Use of Grant Funds for Innovative Program Development

With relatively few exceptions, developmental programs are not the most richly funded programs on community college campuses. In fact, a study by Boylan et al. (1996) has found that although developmental education can be a profit center for many community colleges, this profit is often used to support other, higher cost, academic programs such as health sciences or more expensive vocational programs. In fact, profits from developmental education often help the institution by enabling it to provide important specialized vocational and technical programs that it would not otherwise be possible to support.

Boylan et al. (1996) have also reported that there are many institutions in which developmental programs produce far more revenue than is represented by their funding. Even when the revenues from developmental education dramatically exceed its costs, therefore, developmental programs are likely to have little "venture capital" available for program development.

The CQIN/APQC study (2000) has further documented that the most successful developmental programs responded to this situation by using grant funds for innovation and program improvement. This represents a new finding not previously documented in the literature. It is, nevertheless, informative for those who wish to expand or improve program services without having to rely on institutional resources.

The most common sources of grant funds for developmental education come from Title III, Title IV, and Title V grants from the U.S. Department of Education. Title III grants are designed to strengthen institutions with large numbers of economically disadvantaged students and are funded under various reauthorizations of the Higher Education Act of 1965. Title IV grants provide funds for Talent Search, Upward Bound, Student Support Services, and other programs (subsequently referred to as TRIO programs) designed to enhance educational opportunities for first-generation college students. Title V grants are funded under the most recent reauthorization of this act to support Hispanic-serving institutions.

Many community colleges fund adult basic education and developmental education activities through the Workforce Investment Act (1988) through the Department of Labor. Several community colleges also receive innovation grants from the Fund for the Improvement of Postsecondary Education (FIPSE). In addition to these federal sources of grant funding, there are also a variety of state and local philanthropic foundations and local business and industry grants that fund activities designed to improve educational opportunities in a particular state or region.

Best-practice developmental education programs were aggressive in seeking external grants to support innovation. They did not rely on state

OUACHITA TECHNICAL COLLEGE

allocations, increases in tuition, or institutional resource allocations to refine or enhance their activities. They were, however, careful not to use grant funds to replace "hard" funding of program services.

———∽∼∿—

Oakton Community College has consistently experienced problems in funding its developmental education and learning assistance programs. Over the years, however, faculty and staff of these programs have collaborated with college administrators in seeking federal funds to expand existing activities in support of special populations. For instance, the college used a basic skills grant to enhance learning center support for developmental courses and to improve integration of classroom and learning assistance activities. A TRIO grant enabled the college to expand existing counseling and tutoring activities to serve first-generation college students.

———∽∼∿—

Tips on Use of Grant Funds for Innovation

- Small grants ($500-$2,500) may often be obtained from local businesses. Frequently, a 2 to 3 page letter describing why the funds are needed, what they will be used to accomplish, and how the proposed project will benefit the community are sufficient to obtain such grants.

- In every state, there are a variety of small, little known, philanthropic organizations and foundations. These can be identified through web searches or foundation directories. Because these foundations are not widely known, there is less competition for their financial support. Also, these foundations usually specify that their funding benefit the people of a particular state or region, thus further limiting competition for their funding. Consequently, they can be a good source of funds for special projects and innovations.

- Although external funding represents a good source of support for innovative projects, attention should be given at the outset to how the innovation will be sustained over time should it prove to be successful. Projects that can be self-sustaining after grant funds have expired are particularly attractive to administrators and to funding agencies.

- The most common reason why grant proposals are not funded is that they fail to follow the directions provided in the funding agency's Request for Proposals (RFP). All proposals for external funds should be thoroughly reviewed to insure that the proposal follows the directions listed in the RFP, that it addresses the funding agency's priorities, and that it provides all the information required by the funding agency.

- Before seeking funding from outside agencies, developmental educators should consult with campus officials responsible for grants and development. This will insure that a proposal submitted by the developmental education program does not conflict with some other institutional overture to a particular funding agency.

- Many funding agencies are eager to promote partnerships among educational institutions, particularly high schools and colleges or colleges and universities. The case for a particular project can often be strengthened by establishing partnerships to deliver project activities.

- In seeking external funding it is important to bear in mind that philanthropic organizations fund innovative ideas and solutions. The quality of ideas and solutions described in a funding proposal are far more important than the elegance of program designs.

- The evaluation component is an important part of any funding proposal. Most funding agencies want to see a strong combination of formative and summative methods employed in evaluating the proposed program.

1.9: Integration of Developmental Education and Community Outreach

A major new finding is that strong developmental programs are integrated into colleges' community outreach and workforce development activities (CQIN/APQC, 2000). This is, apparently, a growing trend in colleges and universities (McCabe, 2000).

According to a recent study by the American Association of Community Colleges (Shults, 2000), 47% of public community colleges provide contracted remedial courses to business and industry. The majority of contracted remediation (61%) is designed through collaborative efforts between the institution and the contracting agency. This study also has found that remedial mathematics, reading, and writing, along with ESL, are the courses most frequently offered to local business and industry (Shults, 2000).

The finding that best-practice programs are integrated into the colleges' community outreach is relatively new in the literature and, therefore, has little previous support from recent research. It remains, however, a very strong finding.

Every best-practice program in the study was engaged in some form of community outreach and workforce development effort–usually at several different levels and in several different projects. For instance, they taught courses ranging from basic literacy to technical writing for local business and industry. They were also involved in a variety of community development projects that utilized their skills as teachers, tutors, or counselors.

Although this finding has little previous support in the literature, it does have considerable face validity. Developmental education programs tend to be seen as critical to the institutional mission when they are seen as one of the major solutions available to address workforce and social needs. These programs are, therefore, more likely to be an institutional priority. And, as discussed earlier in this chapter, being an institutional priority contributes to successful developmental education.

Furthermore, the literature consistently reports that adults learn best when instruction is based on realistic examples and relevant issues (Casazza & Silverman, 1996; Cross, 1992; Knowles, 1980; Knowles, 1990). When developmental education faculty and staff engage in community outreach, they are better able to link developmental instruction to issues relevant to local adults.

The developmental education program's profile is raised and its image is enhanced when it has a visible role in the community. Participating in community outreach makes it more likely that developmental education will have local support, particularly from business and community leaders.

Participating in workforce development is an important new role for developmental education in the 21st century. As Robert McCabe points out (2000), "Substantial numbers of people will reach adulthood without the skills necessary for employment in the information age. Effective community college remediation must be there for these individuals. It is their lifeline to the future" (p. 28). Integrating developmental education into workforce development activities not only benefits the local community, but the CQIN/APQC study (2000) indicates that it can also strengthen the developmental program.

———∿∿∿———

The Developmental Studies Program at Durham Technical College in North Carolina has conducted a series of training workshops funded by a local foundation to train public high school teachers in teaching reading across the curriculum. The program has also engaged in a partnership with IBM to teach on-site developmental writing classes to two shifts of line employees. This has served as a model for other collaborative projects with local business and industry.

———∿∿∿———

Tips for Integration of Developmental Education and Community Outreach

- Frequently, it is difficult for community, business, or industry representatives to identify exactly what they expect from collaboration with the local college or university. Nevertheless, if collaboration is to be viewed as successful by all parties, it is essential that expectations be realistic. Developmental educators should, therefore, take care at the outset to insure that everyone involved in collaborative efforts has a realistic understanding of what can and cannot be accomplished through collaboration.
- Formative and summative evaluation processes and measures should be defined and agreed upon at the outset of any collaborative venture. This will insure that everyone involved will know whether or not the venture succeeded and how it might be improved.
- Developmental educators should recognize that the culture of post-secondary education often differs dramatically from the cultures of business, industry, and community service. When discussing collaboration with business, industry, and community representatives, it is important to understand how these cultures differ and how these differences may impact on the design and implementation of collaborative projects.
- Developmental educators should be aware that they are representing their institutions and may even be seen as spokespersons for their

institutions when they are engaging in collaborative efforts with outside agencies. Potential collaborative projects, therefore, should be reviewed by campus administrators and potential institutional stakeholders before entering into negotiations with off-campus agencies.

- Collaborative partnerships between postsecondary institutions and community businesses, industries, or services work best when they focus on the solution of a problem recognized by all those involved. The more clearly and specificly the project focus is identified and communicated at the outset, the better all parties will be able to assess project outcomes.

- It is often useful for developmental programs to establish a "speakers bureau" to talk about developmental education to local business, social, religious, and civic groups. This helps carry the message of developmental education into the community and may often nourish future partnerships.

CHAPTER 2

Program Components

For underprepared students, developmental education frequently represents their major contact with the institution. Their attitudes toward higher education in general and the institution in particular are often determined by their experiences in developmental courses and services. It is essential, therefore, that these courses and services be as accessible, as comprehensive, as user friendly, and as helpful as possible.

For developmental students, life goes on along with—and frequently in competition with—their academic experiences. Developmental educators recognize this.

The most basic concept in developmental education is that students are complete human beings. Their attitudes toward learning, their motivation, their self-concepts, and their confidence have as much or more to do with their success in college as do their academic skills. Consequently, developmental programs should consist of more than just isolated courses and support services. The developmental program should provide a variety of courses, activities, and support services undergirded by a developmental philosophy. Furthermore, these courses, activities, and services should be provided by academic professionals who value and understand the contributions that research can make to improve practice.

The research-based components of exemplary programs described in this chapter represent part of a holistic approach to developmental education. This holistic approach emphasizes systematic development not only for students but also for the faculty and staff involved in the delivery of developmental education.

2.1: Mandatory Assessment and Placement

In order to serve underprepared students, it is first necessary to identify them and determine their skill levels. That is why mandatory assessment of students has long been recognized as a critical initial step in developmental education. In fact, mandatory assessment is so important that 26 states now require it of their public colleges and universities (Russell, 1997).

In order for mandatory assessment to be meaningful, however, it must be supported by mandatory placement. Unfortunately, although practically all community colleges require assessment, many of them do not require students to be placed in courses based on this assessment. Mandatory assessment followed by voluntary placement undermines the entire concept of assessment as a means of promoting student success. As Morante (1989) points out, allowing students to enroll in courses for which they are not prepared is tantamount to promoting failure.

Research has consistently shown that mandatory assessment and placement contributes to student success (McCabe, 2000; McCabe & Day, 1998; Roueche & Roueche, 1999). Yet many community colleges are reluctant to prohibit students from enrolling in courses for which assessment shows they are not prepared.

Some colleges fear that students will leave and attend other institutions if they are prohibited from taking the courses they want. There is, however, no evidence to suggest that this actually takes place.

Others are reluctant to require students to participate in developmental education because they believe that assessment test results are not completely accurate. This, too, is unsupported by any research. There is, of course, a range of measurement error with any placement instrument. But for most of the scientifically developed and better-validated instruments, this error range is around 5%. Roueche and Roueche (1999) note that placement tests "may not be accurate without a doubt, (but) the more common tests are valid indicators that students have a problem"[1] (p. 30).

Still others want evidence that developmental courses actually contribute to student success before they force students to take them. This concern is probably the most valid. As Norton Grubb points out (1999) many developmental courses are dull, poorly taught, and emphasize low-level drill and practice. Many students drop out of or fail these courses simply because of boredom or dissatisfaction with instruction.

Given this, an evaluation of completion rates and grades in developmental courses should be undertaken before requiring placement on the basis of assessment. If more than 50% of the students still enrolled after the

---

[1] The most common placement tests used by community colleges are the ASSET and the COMPASS produced by ACT, and the Computerized Placement Test produced by the Education Testing Service. Many colleges also use institutionally developed assessment instruments to test student mathematics skills.

first month of classes fail to complete a developmental course, the instructional methods and techniques of that course should be examined. Efforts should be made to improve the quality of instruction in these courses before students are forced to take them.

In considering mandatory assessment and placement, it should be noted that, although mandatory assessment was found to be related to student success, mandatory placement was shown to have a slightly negative effect on retention in some cases. Boylan, Bliss, and Bonham (1997) found that mandatory placement was positively correlated with pass rates in community college developmental English and math courses, but they also found that it was somewhat negatively correlated with retention in developmental programs. The authors speculated that where placement was voluntary, the weakest students did not participate in developmental courses. A higher percentage of weaker students were enrolled in developmental courses, thus driving down retention where placement was mandatory.

This, however, should not serve as an argument against mandatory placement. Even though many of the weakest students are not retained by developmental education, it is also unlikely that they would be retained without it. Cross (1976) estimates that only about 10% of students who place in developmental courses would graduate without developmental education intervention. McCabe and Day (1998) speculate that as many as two million students a year would leave postsecondary education if they did not have access to developmental education. To many experts it is senseless to mandate assessment without accompanying this mandate with placement based on the assessment. As Roueche and Roueche point out (1999) "Universities do not hesitate to prohibit students from enrolling in courses for which they are not prepared or have not completed prerequisites; community colleges should do no less" (p. 30).

—⟋⟍⟍—

Trident Technical College in Charleston, South Carolina places great emphasis on assessment. Students who do not have qualifying SAT or ACT scores are required to take a battery of computerized tests in reading, English, arithmetic, and elementary algebra. Cut scores from this testing are based on the competencies identified as being essential to success in college-level courses. Placement is then mandatory based on

discussions with college advisors. Evaluation activities are also
undertaken to insure that the developmental courses are actu-
ally contributing to student success.

———∼∼∼———

Tips for Mandatory Assessment and Placement

- Once an assessment instrument has been selected for use, all those
  involved in developmental education should take the test. This will
  insure that they are familiar with what it does and does not measure
  and it will help them understand its strengths and weaknesses.
- All academic advisors should be provided with a copy of the assessment instrument's technical manual and be required to read it. This
  will help them discuss the instrument with students and enable them
  to interpret and use test results more effectively.
- It should be recognized at the outset that "mandatory" is a relative
  term. No matter what controls are placed on assessment and registration, some students will always "slip through the cracks." It is
  probably impossible to insure that assessment is 100% mandatory.
  Every effort, however, should be made to insure that each student
  who can profit from assessment participates in it.
- Many students place into developmental courses because they lack
  test-taking skills. It is a good idea, therefore, to make free test-taking
  workshops available to students before they take the assessment test.
  This will reduce the number of students who are placed into developmental courses simply because they are unfamiliar with taking
  standardized tests.
- No assessment instrument is 100% accurate for all students. It is
  important, therefore, to provide students with opportunities to challenge test results if they feel they have been misplaced. Such
  challenges may involve retaking the assessment test, participating in
  future academic advising, or taking some alternative test. The opportunity to challenge placement also contributes to students' feelings
  that they have had a fair chance to demonstrate their abilities.
- Students who are mandated into developmental education courses
  should not only be required to register for them but also to participate appropriately in and to attend classes regularly as a condition of

continued enrollment at the institution. This should be made clear at the outset by advisors and reinforced by instructors.

2.2: Systematic Program Evaluation

Few program components are more important than evaluation. Time and again, research has shown that developmental programs undertaking regular and systematic evaluation are more successful than those that either fail to evaluate their activities or evaluate them erratically.

Donovan (1974) reported that developmental programs that evaluated their outcomes were more likely to be successful than those that did not. Cross (1976) found that a systematic evaluation component characterized programs that contributed to student retention. Research by Boylan, Bliss, and Bonham (1997) indicated that programs emphasizing the evaluation of their outcomes were more likely to retain students and to have higher pass rates in developmental courses. Roueche and Roueche (1999) reported that the most successful developmental programs regularly evaluated the outcomes of their efforts. The CQIN/APQC study (2000) reported that all the developmental programs identified as exemplary engaged in ongoing and systematic evaluation activities.

Although most developmental education programs conduct some sort of evaluation, what is done is rarely systematic. Developmental courses, for instance, are almost always evaluated by students. Tutoring programs usually request some sort of feedback from students on the quality of the tutoring experience. Learning laboratories typically gather information on the number of students served and the types of services provided. These activities, however, are rarely part of an overall campus evaluation plan for developmental education. They are rarely coordinated with each other. The results of evaluation are rarely shared with developmental education faculty and staff in order to promote program improvement. They are rarely used systematically for both formative and summative evaluation purposes (Boylan, Bonham, Claxton, & Bliss, 1992).

Systematic evaluation implies that:

- evaluation is done at regular intervals,
- evaluation activities are undertaken as part of a systematic plan,

- evaluation activities are both formative and summative,
- evaluation activities use a variety of measures, and
- evaluation information is shared with a variety of audiences.

As the American Association for Higher Education (1992) points out, assessment works best when it is ongoing, not episodic. This is, perhaps, one of the greatest failings of contemporary evaluations of developmental education (Boylan & Saxon, 1998). They take place at irregular intervals and are not part of some systematic evaluation plan. Furthermore, evaluation results are rarely shared with those who are in the best position to change things as a result of evaluation information.

A systematic evaluation of developmental education activities should be multifaceted. As Boylan, Bonham, White, and George (2000) point out, systematic evaluation should collect data at three levels. At the primary level, it should collect data on the number of courses, hours of tutoring, and students served. This provides a picture of what is actually being done in developmental education. At the secondary level it should collect data on the short-term outcomes of developmental courses such as course completion rates, grades in courses, and semester-to-semester retention. This describes the extent to which developmental education is effective in the short-term. At the tertiary level, it should collect data on the long-term outcomes such as grade point averages, long-term retention, and graduation rates (Boylan, Bonham, White, & George, 2000). This describes how successful developmental education is in the long-term. Combining data from these three levels contributes to a more complete understanding of the entire developmental education process.

Over the years, an "industry standard" has evolved for criteria to be used in the evaluation of developmental education programs (Boylan, Bonham, White, & George, 2000). These criteria include:

- completion rates for developmental courses,
- grades in developmental courses,
- grades obtained in postdevelopmental education curriculum courses in the same subject area,
- retention rates for developmental students,
- grades in courses for which developmental students are tutored,
- student satisfaction with courses and services,

- faculty satisfaction with the skills of students who participate in developmental courses and services, and
- graduation rates for developmental students.

These criteria represent the types of outcomes that developmental educators should explore in evaluating their programs. Because they have become the industry standard, use of these measures also allows individual campuses to compare their outcomes with those of programs at other campuses as well as measure themselves against national standards of performance.

The National Center for Education Statistics (1996) calculated the mean percentage of students successfully completing developmental courses by subject area and institutional type for a national random sample of colleges and universities. The National Study of Developmental Education (Boylan, Bonham, Claxton, & Bliss, 1992) calculated the pass rates of students completing the developmental education sequence who also took the next level course in the same or related subject area. Information from these studies is presented in Tables 1 and 2 as a means of enabling institutions to compare their outcomes with a national standard.

Table 1

Percent of Students Passing Developmental Courses

Within One Year at Various Types of Institutions

Institution Type	Reading	Writing	Mathematics
Public 2-year	72%	79%	74%
Public 4-year	82%	81%	71%
Private 4-year	84%	88%	84%

Table 2

Percent of Students Passing Highest Level Developmental Course

And Taking and Passing First College-Level Course in that Subject

Institution Type	Mathematics	English	Reading*
2-year	65%	88%	77%
4-year	77%	91%	83%

* Note: Students who passed highest level of developmental reading and then passed their first college-level social science course.

—᙭᙭᙭—

The Community College of Denver has developed a systematic program evaluation plan for developmental education that measures a variety of outcomes for those who participate in developmental courses and services. These evaluations are carried out annually by each unit providing developmental courses and services. This evaluation activity is coordinated by the institution's Office of Information Resources and Planning which provides feedback to individual units on their performance.

—᙭᙭᙭—

Tips for Program Evaluation

- Systematic evaluation in developmental education requires that a plan be designed for measurement of program outcomes. To the extent that all faculty and staff—both full-time and part-time—of the program have input into this plan, they are more likely to regard evaluation results as valid.
- Once an evaluation plan for developmental education has been developed, it should be shared with key campus administrators. Administrators are more likely to use evaluation data for decision making when they share in developing and reviewing evaluation plans.
- An important part of any evaluation plan is dissemination. The people to whom evaluation results will be disseminated and the use to which evaluation data will be put should be identified at the outset and be built into the evaluation dissemination plan. Any evaluation plan should be accompanied by a plan for dissemination of evaluation results.
- Evaluation of developmental education does not require the use of complicated statistics. Program outcomes can be accurately described using nothing more than percentages, bar graphs, or pie charts. Reporting of data should be kept simple because most readers of evaluation reports are not statisticians.
- Campus institutional research or assessment officers frequently have a great deal of data that can be used in evaluating developmental education. They also have expertise and experience relevant to program evaluation. Institutional research personnel should, there-

fore, be consulted in designing a program evaluation plan for developmental education.

- Any lengthy evaluation report submitted to campus administrators should be accompanied by an executive summary. The executive summary highlights the methods, findings, and conclusions in two or three pages. This makes it easy for those receiving the report to gain a quick understanding of the major issues under consideration and helps to guide their more thorough review of the report.

2.3: Formative Evaluation for Program Improvement

According to Stake (1967) there are two major types of evaluation: formative and summative. Formative evaluation takes place when evaluation data is used for the purpose of developing or improving courses or services, and summative evaluation takes place when evaluation data is used to measure the outcomes of courses or services at the end of some specified period. Formative evaluation measures the short-term impact of program activities and is used to guide and refine further activities. Formative evaluation, therefore, is the key to improvement for developmental courses and services.

Although the importance of program evaluation cannot be over-emphasized, the use of evaluation data for formative purposes appears to be the most essential aspect of successful program evaluation. It usually takes place as the program or course is being delivered and it is used to improve what is being delivered. Formative evaluation differs from other forms of evaluation in that the primary purpose of formative evaluation is to improve the quality of what is being done. Formative evaluation is not used to determine how well courses or services have accomplished their objectives or to make some final judgment on the effectiveness of courses or services. It is used, exclusively, to promote program improvement.

The most effective formative evaluation is done by the faculty and staff directly involved in the developmental program, usually as a collective group. In fact, one of the strengths of formative evaluation is that it brings together all parties involved in the program to look at what is being done, to decide if it is sufficient, and to make recommendations for revision. In formative evaluation, the people who deliver the services are the people who control what is done as a result of the evaluation. In essence, formative evaluation represents the "grassroots" of outcomes assessment. The people in the "front lines" of developmental education who are best able to make changes based on data are the ones who ought to be most involved in the formative evaluation process.

Unlike other forms of evaluation, therefore, formative evaluation is ongoing. It takes place as services are delivered and as courses are being taught. Successful developmental programs are constantly involved in collecting and analyzing data for formative purposes. Formative evaluation is, therefore, an essential part of the continuous quality improvement process.

Boylan and Saxon (1998) found that programs in Texas colleges and universities using formative evaluation for program improvement had higher rates of course completion and retention. In fact, an emphasis on formative evaluation characterized all the most effective developmental programs in Texas. The National Study of Developmental Education reported similar results. Students in programs that used evaluation data for formative purposes consistently had higher grades than students in programs that did not use evaluation data for formative purposes (Boylan, Bonham, Claxton, & Bliss, 1992). Similar findings were reported in the CQIN/APQC study (2000).

———

Oakton Community College in Des Plaines, Illinois places a great deal of emphasis on formative evaluation. In so doing, campus developmental educators work closely with the institution's Office of Research, Curriculum, and Planning to guide and develop formative studies. A primary measure used for formative evaluation at Oakton is performance of students in subsequent courses following developmental education.

A particularly interesting formative evaluation project at Oakton has been undertaken in collaboration with DePaul University. Oakton is a feeder school for DePaul and the two institutions have collaborated to determine how well Oakton transfer students fare once they enroll at DePaul. Results from this study guide curriculum development for compositon course at Oakton.

———

Tips for Formative Evaluation

- If formative evaluation is to result in program improvement, it must be shared, reviewed, and analyzed by those people who can have the most impact on developmental education. This includes the administrators, faculty, and staff who work with developmental education. These individuals should be the ones to plan program revisions based on evaluation results.

- Program personnel are more likely to be influenced by formative evaluation if they are involved in developing the evaluation plan. Those who are most likely to be influenced by the results of formative evaluation should be part of the team planning formative evaluation activities.

- Baseline data is frequently useful for formative evaluation purposes. This data can be obtained by averaging the past 3 years of outcomes measures to obtain a baseline. For instance, if the average pass rates for English 090 during the past 3 years are 70%, this forms a baseline against which to compare future outcomes. If pass rates fall below this rate in any given year, action should be taken to determine what may have caused the drop and what may be changed to improve pass rates.

- It is important to remember that a point of diminishing returns will eventually be reached in using baseline data. For instance, if 90% of students are passing English 090 and this figure remains stable for 2 or 3 years, there is probably not much more that can reasonably be done to improve the English 090 pass rate outcomes. Revision and improvement efforts should then be focused on some other aspect of the program.

- Students can be a valuable source of information for formative evaluation and program improvement. Results from student questionnaires, surveys, or exit interviews should be included in any data collection effort for formative evaluation.

- Part-time or adjunct instructors often teach a substantial number of the courses offered by any developmental program. Consequently, they have a major influence on the outcomes of developmental courses. Because of this, they must be involved in the design and review of formative evaluation data.

2.4: Emphasis on Professional Development

As Mark Twain once said, "Training is everything. The peach was once the bitter almond. Cauliflower is nothing but cabbage with a college education." So it is with developmental education programs.

The developmental programs that emphasize professional development for faculty and staff are generally more successful than programs without such an emphasis. Casazza and Silverman (1996) argue that it is essential "that staff have ongoing professional development activities to help them grow and stay current with information in the field" (p.79). It is this professional development that insures those who work with developmental students are aware of the best of current research, theory, and practice. This increases the likelihood that those who work with developmental students utilize the best available theories, models, and techniques in teaching courses and providing services.

Boylan, Bonham, Claxton, and Bliss, (1992) found that tutoring, advising, and instructional programs with a strong professional development component had greater rates of student retention and better performance in developmental courses than programs without such an emphasis. In fact, using regression analysis, this study found that training was one of the most important variables contributing to the success of any component of developmental education. No matter what component of developmental education was being studied, an emphasis on training and professional development improved its outcomes. Boylan, Bonham, Claxton, and Bliss (1992) found this to be true for tutoring, advising, and instruction. When professional development was emphasized, the outcomes of each of these components improved. Boylan and Saxon (1998), for instance, found that developmental instruction programs emphasizing professional development had higher postdevelopmental education pass rates on a standardized state competency test. Boylan, Bonham, and Bliss (1997) found that the outcomes of tutoring programs were enhanced when an emphasis on tutor training was present.

In the most successful developmental programs, training and professional development is a priority. Faculty and staff working with developmental students are supported and encouraged to attend conferences, training institutes, and graduate courses. Those who participate in such activities are encouraged to share what they have learned with their colleagues in formal and informal settings.

An emphasis on professional development may employ a wide range of strategies. Having faculty and staff read and discuss books and articles in the field is an inexpensive but effective way of promoting professional development. Having colleagues with expertise in specific models or techniques run workshops for developmental educators is also inexpensive. Bringing in external consultants to run workshops and seminars is a more expensive but, nevertheless, effective means of promoting professional development. Attending conferences, participating in training institutes, or enrolling in graduate courses are also effective professional development activities.

In designing and delivering professional development, it is important to bear in mind that ongoing, long-term professional development programs are the most effective. The "one shot" professional development activity is far less effective than a sustained and intensive series of professional developmental activities undertaken over time (Garret, Porter, Desimone, Birman, & Yoon, 2001). Furthermore, effective professional development should involve a combination of general instructional or service delivery strategies and those which are subject specific (Garret, Porter, Desimone, Birman, & Yoon, 2001).

—⟋⟍⟍—

Faculty members of the General College of the University of Minnesota are expected to engage in scholarly research and publication as part of university requirements for promotion and tenure. The college, however, takes the position that the academic discipline of these faculty is developmental education and learning assistance. As a result, General College faculty are expected to focus their research on issues relevant to developmental education and learning assistance. In support of this, the college not only provides its faculty with funding to attend professional conferences in developmental education, it also provides release time for scholarship and professional development activities.

—⟋⟍⟍—

Tips for Professional Development

- Professional development may be promoted by having each developmental education faculty and staff member identify areas where they wish to develop their knowledge at the beginning of each academic year. They then negotiate a professional development plan with their supervisors, and fulfillment of this plan becomes part of their portfolio for salary, tenure, and promotion decisions.

- Local campus expertise should not be overlooked when planning professional development. Campus student affairs and counseling staff are often highly trained in skills and techniques that are useful to developmental educators. The campus admissions office can provide tips on marketing programs and services. Faculty who have been particularly effective in implementing innovative teaching strategies can provide workshops for others. All these resources can provide cost-effective faculty development activities.

- The institution has a right to expect that those who attend will bring back and share what they have learned with others if it pays for faculty and staff to attend professional conferences or institutes. This sharing may be in the form of a memo to colleagues, informal presentations at staff meetings, or contributions of materials to the program's professional development library.

- Programs that value professional development frequently have a professional development library for use by faculty and staff. This library may be nothing more than a series of shelves or filing cabinets in the learning center where professional periodicals and books are housed, or it may be a room or section in the campus library. The key, however, is that those involved in developmental education have a specific place they can go to obtain materials and information relevant to professional development.

- The importance of professional development for part-time and adjunct faculty cannot be overlooked because these faculty often teach a substantial number of developmental courses,. Part-time and adjunct faculty should be included in all local professional development activities. They should also be supported with release time and funds for conference attendance whenever possible.

- Consideration should be given to scheduling on-campus professional development activities at times when part-time and adjunct faculty can attend.

2.5: Provision of Tutoring

Tutoring is one of the oldest forms of developmental education intervention. According to Maxwell (1997), tutoring has been provided for underprepared college students since the earliest days of higher education in the United States. The first tutors in North America were ministers who provided tutoring in Greek and Latin for those who aspired to enter Harvard College (Brubacher & Rudy, 1976). In the present day, tutoring is also a key component of most successful developmental programs (Casazza & Silverman, 1996).

Typically, tutoring is provided either through a centralized developmental program or through an academic support services unit such as a learning assistance center or a learning lab associated with an academic department. Although both group and individual tutoring can be effective, individual tutoring appears to be the most dominant form of tutoring provided to developmental students (Boylan, Bonham, Claxton, & Bliss, 1992).

The most common methods of providing tutoring are the use of peer or professional tutors. Developmental education programs in both colleges and universities frequently use part-time peer tutors. Community colleges use full-time professional tutors about twice as frequently as universities (Boylan, Bonham, Bliss, & Claxton, 1992). However, there is, as yet, no evidence to suggest that either peer or professional tutors are more effective (Maxwell, 1997). For administrative purposes, however, full-time tutors are usually more convenient.

At a minimum, successful developmental programs provide tutoring in English, reading, study strategies, and mathematics. It is not atypical, however, for developmental programs to provide tutoring in other subjects such as the social, behavioral, or biological sciences.

Regardless of what sort of tutoring is being provided or where it is housed, the most important aspect of successful tutoring is tutor training. The provision of tutoring by well-trained tutors, as opposed to untrained or marginally trained tutors, is what separates successful tutoring programs from mediocre tutoring programs (Boylan, Bliss, & Bonham, 1997; Casazza & Silverman, 1996; Maxwell, 1997).

According to Casazza and Silverman (1996), successful tutor training programs usually provide a combination of preservice and in-service training for tutors. Typical components of successful tutor training programs include such things as:

- learning theory,
- metacognition,
- motivation,
- counseling/interviewing,
- group dynamics, and
- adult learning models.

MacDonald (1994) also emphasized the importance of training tutors in communication skills, particularly cross-cultural communication. The National Study of Developmental Education (Boylan, Bonham, Claxton, & Bliss, 1992), however, indicated that record keeping and program procedures were the topics most emphasized in typical tutor training programs.

One of the most effective ways of improving tutor training is to participate in the College Reading and Learning Association Tutor Training Certification Program. This program provides guidelines for tutor training and allows tutoring programs to certify tutors at varying levels of expertise depending upon how much training is provided in recommended topic areas (College Reading and Learning Association, undated a, undated b).

———∞———

The Tutoring Center at Bucks County Community College in Newton, Pennsylvania offers tutoring to all students attending the institution. However, 28% of all the center's tutoring hours are provided to developmental students.

At the beginning of each semester, developmental students accompanied by their instructors attend an orientation to the Tutoring Center. This insures that both students and faculty are aware of the center's services and procedures. The Tutoring Center has a director and two supervisors: one for mathematics and one for writing. The supervisors oversee

tutoring activities and coordinate training. All tutors partici-
pate in training at least through Level I of the College Reading
and Learning Association's Tutor Training Certification
Program.

———✦———

Tips for Provision of Tutoring

- It is always a good idea to have faculty recommend tutors from among students who have been successful in their courses. This not only provides a measure of quality control in the tutor selection process, it also helps make faculty feel that they are a part of the developmental education effort.

- Many programs provide business cards for their primary tutors. The card provides tutees with the tutor's name, telephone number, and/or email address so that they can contact the tutor easily when they need help. The reverse of the card may also be used for scheduling future tutoring appointments. Providing business cards may also contribute to a sense of professionalism among tutors.

- Tutoring schedules should reflect the reality of students' lives. This means that tutoring centers should be open on weekends and evenings to provide services to students. Surveys of students partic-ipating and those not participating in tutoring can be used to help determine the best schedule for tutoring services.

- Whenever possible, tutors should experience at least a minimum of training before working with students. This can be accomplished through preservice training prior to the beginning of each semester. If possible, tutors should be paid or provided with some other form or reward for participation in preservice training. Universities, for instance, frequently provide training through credit-bearing elective courses.

- It is often helpful to pair new tutors with more experienced tutors for mentoring purposes. Formal and informal mentoring by experienced tutors can be a valuable part of the tutor training program.

- There is, as yet, little evidence to suggest that matching students and tutors by gender or ethnicity improves tutoring outcomes. Nevertheless, the presence of diversity among the tutoring staff makes a statement that diversity is valued in the developmental education program.

- It is often a more important motivation for tutors to be a valued member of a team than for them to receive pay or course credit. Anything that contributes to tutor morale and sense of belonging is a valuable activity. Examples of such activities include providing t-shirts for tutors, holding picnics or parties for tutors, participating in intramural sports as a unit, or going on trips as a group to encourage tutor morale.

2.6: Involvement in Professional Associations

The CQIN/APQC study (2000) found that faculty and staff in best-practice developmental programs, were involved in developmental education professional associations. This is a relatively new finding. It is supported in previous research only by Boylan and Saxon (1998). In a study of Texas colleges and universities they found that in programs in which faculty were actively involved in state and local developmental education professional associations, students were more likely to be retained through their first academic year.

Although the support for this finding is limited, the concept certainly makes sense. Participation in professional associations is related to professional development which, as discussed earlier, is correlated with program success. Faculty and staff who are involved in developmental education professional associations are more likely to learn about current techniques in the field. They are more likely to participate in discussions of various techniques and learn their strengths and weaknesses. They are more likely to have access to others who have tried these techniques and can provide practical advice on implementation. They are also more likely to have access to a network of other professionals who can provide support, encouragement, and advice on an ongoing basis.

Furthermore, participation in developmental education professional associations helps to provide focus and motivation for improved practice. Professional associations typically provide standards for the evaluation of practice (Council for the Advancement of Standards, 1986; Thayer, 1995).

Access to such standards provides direction to program improvement activities through the application of these standards.

Participation in developmental education professional associations encourages professional behaviors such as the use of research and theory to guide practice, adherence to professional ethics, and the documentation of outcomes. Participation in professional associations also promotes sustained interest in developmental education, thus making it more likely that those who teach developmental courses are also those who are most interested in doing so.

According to the CQIN/APQC study (2000), the professional associations in which faculty and staff of best-practice programs were most likely to belong included:

- the College Reading and Learning Association,
- the National Academic Advising Association,
- the National Association for Developmental Education,
- the National Orientation Directors Association, and
- the National Tutoring Association.

Other major professional associations in the field include the College Reading Association, the National College Learning Center Association, and the New York College Learning Skills Association.

Anecdotal evidence suggests that the exact nature of professional involvement matters less than the fact that it takes place. Faculty and staff participation in any professional association concerned with developmental education appears to have a salutary effect on the outcomes of developmental education activities (Boylan & Saxon, 1998; CQIN/APQC, 2000). However, it is reasonable to assume that greater benefits may result when the professional associations developmental education faculty and staff participate in are related to developmental education and learning assistance.

—⚬⚬⚬—

The learning assistance and developmental programs at Harding University in Searcy, Arkansas have a strong commitment to participation in professional associations. Practically all those involved in developmental education and learning assistance belong to the Arkansas Association for Developmental Education (ArkADE) and many are members of

*the National Association for Developmental Education
(NADE). Many of their staff have served as officers in state and
national professional associations and several have participated in the Kellogg Institute for the Training and Certification
of Developmental Educators. Their learning center staff also
participate in TRIO organizations and attend student support
services conferences and workshops. Their tutoring personnel
are involved in the National Tutoring Association. As a result of
their professional involvement, the tutoring program at
Harding University was one of the first to receive certification
from the National Association for Developmental Education.*

Tips for Involvement in Professional Associations

- State developmental education and learning assistance associations provide a relatively cheap and easily accessible source of profes-sional involvement. The National Association for Developmental Education and the College Reading and Learning Association have local chapters in practically every state in the union. Contact infor-mation for state chapters is usually provided in these associations' newsletters.

- There are also many state organizations devoted to the disciplines represented in developmental education as well as to related areas, such as adult basic education or English as a Second Language, in addition to developmental education professional associations. These associations also provide valuable resources for professional involvement.

- Many national and state professional associations have discount membership fees for adjunct or part-time faculty. They also have dis-count conference fees for adjunct faculty and graduate students. This provides a relatively inexpensive way of getting part-time faculty and staff involved in professional associations.

- Developmental education personnel should be rewarded for their participation if involvement in professional associations is expected of them. Participation in professional associations should, therefore, be considered in salary, tenure, and promotion decisions.

- State professional associations are always looking for institutions to host their conferences. Hosting a state professional group makes it easy for campus personnel to participate and get involved in the state professional association. It also helps the campus develop its statewide network in developmental education.
- Group presentations at local professional conferences can be a useful way of encouraging professional involvement. Most state and local professional associations are eager to have members present at their conferences and may even provide fee waivers as a way of promoting such presentations.

2.7: Adjunct Faculty as a Resource for Developmental Education

According to Boylan, Bonham, and Bliss (1994), over 60% of the nation's community college developmental courses are taught by adjunct or part-time faculty. Similar findings have been reported in a recent American Association of Community Colleges study indicating that over 65% of those teaching developmental courses are part-time (Shults, 2000). This suggests that adjunct faculty have an enormous impact on the quality of teaching and learning encountered by developmental students.

Furthermore, the literature reported no evidence that adjunct faculty were any less successful in teaching developmental courses than full-time faculty. The National Study of Developmental Education (Boylan, Bonham, Claxton, & Bliss, 1992) found that there was no significant difference between the outcomes of developmental courses taught by full-time faculty and those taught by part-time faculty.

Differences in overall outcomes only appeared when a program relied predominantly on adjunct faculty to teach developmental courses. In a study of Texas college and university developmental education, Boylan and Saxon (1998) found that institutions in which 70% or more of the developmental courses were taught by adjunct faculty commonly exhibited unacceptably low pass rates in developmental courses. They also found that institutions with the highest percentages of adjuncts teaching developmental courses had the lowest postdevelopmental education pass rates on the state-mandated TASP test (Boylan & Saxon, 1998).

Although best-practice programs identified in the CQIN/APQC study (2000) relied on adjunct faculty to deliver a significant number of developmental courses, only about 50% of their developmental courses were taught by adjunct faculty in these programs. Best-practice institutions, therefore, had a substantially lower incidence of adjunct utilization in developmental education than the national average.

Resistance to over-reliance on adjuncts also characterized the most successful programs in a study of Texas developmental education. In this study, adjuncts typically taught fewer than half the developmental courses in programs with the highest pass rates on a state-mandated test (Boylan & Saxon, 1998).

When best-practice programs did use adjuncts to teach developmental courses, they were considered a valued program resource. Only adjuncts who expressed a desire to teach developmental courses were hired for this role, and a variety of support mechanisms were provided to help them do so successfully. Manuals and orientation programs were provided for adjunct faculty. Adjunct faculty were encouraged to participate in departmental meetings and participate as full members of the developmental program. Adjunct faculty were also provided with ongoing professional development through workshops and conference attendance. In essence, the most effective programs provided adjunct faculty with the same opportunities as full-time faculty.

Best-practice institutions frequently provided mentoring programs for adjuncts in which full-time faculty worked individually with adjuncts to provide support, encouragement, and advice. In general, developmental programs using adjunct faculty were most successful when the adjuncts were fully integrated into the program and considered as valuable assets to the program.

—⟋⟍⟍—

At Durham Technical College, adjunct instructors have access to the same professional development funds as all other faculty. Grant funds are also used to provide stipends for adjunct faculty to participate in college-wide orientation programs and to attend off-campus professional development activities. The college provides a detailed instructor's manual for adjunct faculty in each developmental education discipline. These manuals not only provide information on grading, exit

competencies, and referral guidelines, they also include guide-
lines for interpreting results from assessment instruments.

—⟩⟨⟨⟩—

Tips on Utilizing Adjunct Faculty

- Adjunct faculty teaching developmental courses should be invited to attend all meetings of the developmental education faculty. They should also be involved in all professional development workshops for developmental educators. This will encourage them to view themselves as part of the overall campus developmental education effort.
- Adjunct faculty should also be invited to all departmental or program social and recreational activities. This will contribute to their feelings of inclusion.
- It is often useful for senior faculty to provide mentoring for adjunct faculty. Mentors should assist in orienting adjuncts to the college, be available to offer guidance, and help adjuncts resolve whatever classroom or teaching problems they encounter when they are provided to adjunct faculty. Such mentoring often takes place informally, but it is more effective when it takes place as part of a structured mentoring program for adjuncts rather than on an ad hoc basis.
- Developmental program personnel are well advised to develop a resource manual for adjunct faculty teaching developmental courses. This manual should include such things as orientation information, the goals and objectives of developmental education, academic policies and procedures, sources of assistance for faculty, and sources of referral for students. It should also include a selection of articles relevant to teaching developmental students as well as a bibliography of useful references.
- Adjunct faculty should be provided with a selection of articles or books of readings relevant to teaching developmental students as well as a bibliography of useful references. Review and discussion of these materials should represent part of the orientation process for adjuncts.
- The ranks of full-time faculty are filled with those who started out as adjuncts. Unfortunately, the processes by which adjuncts become full-time faculty are often vague, haphazard, and filled with

uncertainty. Adjuncts who are interested in teaching full-time should have the path to full-time employment made clear to them. They should also receive counseling to assist them in taking that path productively or be encouraged to seek full-time employment elsewhere if they are not likely to qualify for a full-time position at their current institution. This not only contributes positively to the morale of adjunct faculty, it also encourages greater commitment to the institution.

2.8: Student Performance Monitoring by Faculty and Advisors

Monitoring student performance is an important component of successful developmental programs (Casazza & Silverman, 1996; Maxwell, 1997). In the best developmental programs, however, the monitoring of students is a collaborative responsibility of faculty members and advising staff (CQIN/APQC, 2000; Roueche & Roueche, 1999).

This collaboration enables the developmental program to address a combination of students' affective and cognitive needs. As Bloom (1976) points out, academic or cognitive ability accounts for only about half of a student's success in schooling. The other half is accounted for by a variety of affective factors such as motivation, attitudes toward learning, or willingness to seek help. Faculty members are well equipped to monitor students' cognitive needs, and advisors are well equipped to monitor students' affective needs. Because of this, a synergistic effect often results from collaboration of faculty and advisors.

Faculty can identify students' needs for tutoring, study skills, or drill and practice. Advisors can identify students' needs for time management workshops, support services, or counseling. By working together, they can deal with "the whole student" and provide comprehensive intervention.

The most common example of such collaboration is an "early warning system" by which faculty identify students who may need extra help early in the semester. These students are then referred to an academic advisor who meets with them, discusses their problems, and recommends various solutions. The solutions may range from extra tutoring to accessing the campus day care center. The advisor then makes appropriate referrals and monitors students to insure that they actually follow up on whatever solutions are recommended. Advisors then report the results of their meetings with students to the faculty member who made the referral. Frequently advisors will recommend specific actions to faculty that may help improve a student's performance or request the faculty member's continued help in monitoring student progress.

In many cases, the same advisors may work with students throughout their enrollment in the developmental education program. This allows them to build relationships with students and gain a better understanding of each student's goals, objectives, problems, and needs.

Many colleges and universities also provide special monitoring programs for students judged to be "at risk." In these programs a variety of indicators are used to identify students at risk of failure. These indicators include such things as late registration, extremely low scores on assessment instruments, frequent absenteeism, lack of fluency in English, or a history of educational problems. Students identified by these indicators as being at risk are required to meet certain conditions such as regular attendance at tutoring or meeting with advisors or faculty on a regular basis.

In monitoring at-risk students, it is particularly important that collaborative monitoring of students be initiated early in each semester. Kulik, Kulik, and Schwalb (1983) have found that college programs for high-risk students were more successful when they began their interventions as early as possible in students' academic careers. Similar findings also have been reported by Casazza and Silverman (1996) and McCabe and Day (1998). Early intervention appears to be a key to the success of monitoring activities in developmental education.

———⟋⟍⟍⟍——

At the General College of the University of Minnesota, all faculty receive a data base at the beginning of each semester that lists all students enrolled in their courses along with the students' and the advisors' contact information. Academic alerts are sent to advisors during the first week for students who have not attended classes, do not meet the course prerequisites, or have exhibited some difficulty such as paying for textbooks. The advisors then meet with students, attempt to resolve the problem or make referrals, and then report back to the instructor who issued the alert. At midsemester, every

OUACHITA TECHNICAL COLLEGE

student in every course is described by instructors in a formal midsemester review form, and this information is shared with advisors.

—⚬⚬⚬—

Tips on Monitoring Student Performance

- It is useful to have a checklist of potential problems to guide early discussions when advisors meet with students early in the semester. This checklist may include questions to determine if students are receiving appropriate financial aid, purchasing the textbooks for their classes, missing any classes, or experiencing any problems with their class schedule and their work schedule. This checklist insures that information is obtained that might not normally be volunteered by students.

- It is often valuable to use contracts for working with students who are on academic probation. Such contracts describe what actions students will take in order to improve their academic performance and how these actions will be evaluated. The advisor then meets biweekly with students to monitor the terms of the contract.

- It is usually helpful for advisors to brief students on academic terms, policies, and procedures during meetings with students. Developmental students seldom know the meaning of terms such as "section number," "withdrawal passing/failing," "incomplete," "grade point average," and "credit hours and quality points." Yet these things have an enormous impact on students' status in college. It is also helpful for developmental education faculty to review and describe these terms occasionally in class to reinforce what advisors may have said.

- Many colleges and universities have experienced success in using peer mentors to help monitor student performance. The key in using peer advisors to work with developmental students is that these advisors be carefully selected and very well trained in such things as interviewing skills, academic policies and procedures, and advising ethics.

- It is advisable for institutions to be informed about the College Reading and Learning Association's international certification program for mentors. Participation in this program can be used to develop and strengthen training programs for mentors. Information on this program may be obtained from the Tutoring and Learning Center, 300 Library, UTEP, El Paso, TX 79968.

- Student performance monitoring usually involves the gathering of personal data on students. Those involved in the monitoring process, therefore, should be fully cognizant of the institution's legal obligations to maintain student privacy.

2.9: Developmental Philosophy as a Guide to Program Activities

In one of the earliest studies of developmental education, Donovan (1974) found that successful programs were guided by a clearly stated and explicit developmental philosophy that governed day-to-day delivery of courses and services. This philosophy was grounded in the principles of student development and developmental psychology.

Programs in which such a philosophy guided actions had greater retention rates than those without such a philosophy (Donovan, 1974). Kiemig (1983) argued that a developmental philosophy was essential if the organization, administration, and delivery of courses and services was to be integrated into the institutional mainstream. Roueche and Roueche (1987, 1999) also found that the best-practice institutions they studied were guided by a holistic philosophy of student development.

The basic tenets of such a philosophy are described by Casazza and Silverman (1996):

> If we look back at the belief system that many practitioners of developmental education and learning assistance share, we find that one major theme emerges: placing the learner at the center of our practice. Closely aligned with this learner-centered approach is an understanding of the word developmental. The word denotes an educational process that begins with a determination of where learners are, what they want to achieve, and how to help them realize their greatest potential as they work toward their goals. (p.260)

The CQIN/APQC (2000) study also found that best-practice developmental programs consistently emphasized such a common set of beliefs about developmental students. These beliefs were both holistic and developmental. They recognized students as total beings with both affective and cognitive characteristics shaping their attitudes and behaviors. They valued the notion that courses and activities should focus on the learner. In best-practice institutions, these beliefs were reflected in the program's mission statements, goals and objectives, policies and procedures, as well as the behaviors of faculty and staff.

Most of the time, these beliefs were stated as a set of values that comprised a program's philosophy. Frequently, such statements were included in courses syllabi and displayed prominently in program classrooms and laboratories. In essence, they reflected a set of shared understandings about the role and purpose of developmental education and the centrality of the student to developmental practice.

Faculty and staff not only "talk the talk" but also "walk the walk" when all those involved in a developmental education program are guided by a holistic developmental philosophy. Students are generally treated consistently in all aspects of their participation in the program. They are provided with environments that value them as individuals. Learning takes place in settings that are nonthreatening. Educational and policy decisions are typically made with students' best interests in mind.

Furthermore, by focusing on shared beliefs a professional identity for developmental educators is maintained. This professional identity helps those outside of developmental education to understand it better and enhances the role of developmental education in the campus community. For all these reasons, the identification of and adherence to a holistic developmental philosophy promotes effective developmental education.

—⚬⚬⚬—

Austin Community College developmental educators have developed a philosophy that undergirds all program activities. This philosophy states:

> As developmental educators, we believe in maximizing the potential of our students and ourselves. We strive to achieve and maintain excellence in all our teaching and learning endeavors because we believe in all students' right to excellent postsecondary

educational experiences. It is our mission to help students overcome any barriers that would hinder their personal and academic successes.

We create a learning environment in which faculty employ the best practices in their field, promote individual initiative, honor diversity, empower independent learning, and encourage risk taking. As developmental educators, we use teaching strategies emphasizing active learning, problem solving, and critical thinking while we model a lifelong commitment to learning. (Austin Community College, 1998)

Tips for Developing and Using a Developmental Philosophy

- A developmental philosophy is difficult for faculty and staff to describe or act upon unless they understand basic concepts of human development. All faculty and staff working with developmental students, therefore, should be oriented to the principles of human development. This can take place through the orientation of new faculty, through departmental meetings, or through required readings.
- A program philosophy is, essentially, a statement of those things that program personnel hold to be true about students and about teaching and learning. It is often helpful, therefore, to begin developing a philosophy statement by having faculty and staff write down a list of those things they consider to be true about developmental students and developmental instruction.
- A philosophy statement usually incorporates a set of beliefs about developmental students and the ways in which they should be served. It is important, therefore, that faculty and staff have opportunities to discuss their beliefs about students and services and to establish a set of shared values concerning developmental education.
- A statement of philosophy to guide developmental education should not be something that is written and then filed and forgotten. It should be shared regularly with faculty, staff, and students. It should also be reviewed periodically and revised if necessary.

- Once a philosophy for guiding developmental education is developed, it should be widely disseminated to those involved in developmental education and to those who have a stake in the campus-wide developmental education effort. It should also be prominently posted so that faculty, staff, and students can reference it regularly.
- The purpose of a statement of philosophy is to guide actions. It is essential that the actions of program personnel reflect the program philosophy. A lack of consistency between stated values and faculty and staff behaviors may have a negative impact on student attitudes toward the program.

2.10: Integration of Classrooms and Laboratories

One of the major findings of the National Study of Developmental Education was that programs in which classrooms and laboratories were fully integrated had significantly higher pass rates in developmental courses than programs in which there was little integration (Boylan, Bonham, Claxton, & Bliss, 1992). This was reaffirmed in a 1998 study of developmental education in Texas (Boylan & Saxon, 1998) which found higher postdevelopmental education pass rates on a state mandated test for programs that integrated classrooms and laboratories. Maxwell (1997) pointed out that the effectiveness of laboratory-based tutoring was often related to the extent that laboratory tutors worked closely with instructors. The integration of classrooms and laboratories was also noted by McCabe (2000) as one of the hallmarks of successful developmental education programs.

The integration of classrooms and laboratories appears to be an essential component of successful developmental programs. Nevertheless, observation suggests that a surprising number of colleges and universities provide laboratories to support classrooms but never bother to insure that their activities are coordinated with one another. Instead, they allow classrooms and laboratories to operate independently of one another.

This was not the case with best-practice institutions. The CQIN/APQC (2000) found that best-practice institutions went to great lengths to insure the integration of classrooms and laboratories.

Classrooms and laboratories cannot be assumed to be integrated just because they exist or because students taking classes occasionally use laboratories. Just because an instructor may mention the laboratory and encourage students to use it, it does not mean that the laboratory is integrated with the classroom. Integration implies a much more concerted effort to insure that what goes on in the classroom is clearly connected and specifically supported by what goes on in the laboratory.

Integrated classroom activities and laboratories are characterized by the way in which they are coordinated with each other. Specifically:

- Integration is present when the instructor consults laboratory personnel in developing a particular course to determine how laboratory activities can support that course.
- Integration is present when laboratory materials or activities are directly related to specific course goals and objectives.
- Integration is present when students are required to participate in specific laboratory activities as part of their course assignments.
- Integration is present when laboratory activities count as part of students' grades.
- Integration is present when laboratories are in reasonably close proximity to the courses they will support.

When these characteristics are present, laboratories are likely to have a greater impact in their support of instruction. Without these characteristics, the investments made by institutions in laboratory personnel, equipment, materials, and software are unlikely to have the maximum desired effect on student performance. For example, research (Boylan, Bonham, Claxton, & Bliss, 1992) indicates that laboratory support of courses have a greater impact on student performance when they are in close proximity to each other. This probably suggests that students are more likely to use laboratories when they are near their classrooms.

Most best-practice institutions in the CQIN/APQC (2000) study not only provided laboratories for instruction, they expected instructional and laboratory personnel to work together in a variety of ways. Frequently, laboratory personnel regularly attended meetings of the academic department that originated courses they were supporting. Often, laboratory sections were scheduled and printed out on students' class schedules along with their class meeting times. All of these activities helped to promote the integration of classrooms and laboratories.

—⟋⟍—

At Delgado Community College in New Orleans all developmental students have access to laboratories in each basic skills discipline. All laboratories are closely coordinated with the instructors in each discipline. Laboratories provide tutoring and self-paced computerized instruction. Both reading and conversation laboratories are provided for ESL students as well as computer-assisted instruction in English. An interesting feature of the reading laboratory is that it provides an extensive library of paperback books, and students are encouraged to check these out regularly.

—⟋⟍—

Tips on Integration of Classrooms and Laboratories

- The best time to plan coordination between laboratory and classroom activities is when a course is being designed. Utilization of laboratories should be determined as part of the instructional design process.
- Many colleges and universities use computer laboratories for instructional support. This works best when instructors who will send students to the laboratories actually review the software available there and work through the computerized activities and tests themselves.
- Instructors at many institutions use the laboratory for testing. Rather than administer tests in class, students can schedule their own testing times in the laboratory and have their tests proctored by laboratory personnel.
- Adjuncts teaching developmental courses should be oriented to instructional laboratories and required to meet with laboratory personnel and familiarize themselves with laboratory materials and equipment.
- Instructional laboratories are most effective when they are located in close proximity to the classrooms they serve. This should be considered in facilities planning and renovation.

- The purpose of instructional laboratories should not be to replicate instruction. Laboratories should provide activities that supplement instruction and appeal to a wide variety of learning styles.
- Faculty expectations for student utilization of laboratories should be written into every developmental education course syllabus. This helps reinforce for students the notion that laboratory participation is an integral part of course work.

CHAPTER 3

Instructional Practices

Among the variables over which developmental educators have control, the quality of classroom instruction is the single most important contributor to the success of developmental students. Instructors cannot control students' social or economic backgrounds nor can they have much influence on their work or home life. But they can control what is done in the classroom. The National Study of Developmental Education (Boylan, Bonham, Claxton, & Bliss, 1992) found that no program organizational model or component had as much impact on student academic performance as did the quality of instruction.

Quality of instruction refers not only to delivery methods but also to classroom organization, management, and environment. Instructors should bear in mind that practically everything they do in the classroom has some impact on student learning. It is essential, therefore, that instructional activities be carefully planned, diligently managed, and thoughtfully delivered.

The best practices described in this chapter represent a combination of instructional design, organization, and delivery. There are many models, methods, and techniques that will contribute to quality instruction. Those noted here are the ones having the strongest support in research, literature, and practice for contributing to quality developmental instruction.

3.1: Develop Learning Communities

Following extensive research using data from the Cooperative Institutional Research Program, Astin (1993) found that membership in one or more college communities is a critical factor in student development as well as retention. A consequence of this is that aggressive efforts to involve students in communities should contribute to increased retention.

Tinto (1997) found that the use of learning communities for instruction contributed to improved student grades and enhanced retention. Tinto also found that students learn more from courses that are integrated into a community than they do from isolated courses (Tinto, 1998). Studies of learning communities at selected community colleges indicated that their use improved students' attitudes toward learning (Tinto, 1998). Research at Sandhills Community College (McCabe & Day, 1998) demonstrated that the use of learning communities resulted in a dramatic increase in students' persistence in developmental English and reading courses. Langer (2001), found that the performance of low achieving students increased in environments where there were frequent opportunities for students to interact with and learn from each other. Several of the best-practice programs in the CQIN/APQC (2000) study relied on learning communities as a delivery structure for developmental education.

Instructional learning communities are based on the assumption that the classroom is not only a community, but the only academic community that many students in community colleges or commuter institutions are likely to encounter in their lives. It is important, therefore, to make greater use of the classroom as the place to involve students in the academic culture and to help them understand the rewards and expectations of academe. In a learning community, the classroom not only becomes a place where teaching occurs but also becomes a community in which students learn to learn.

Learning communities link courses and groups of students so that "students encounter learning as a shared rather than isolated experience" (Tinto, 1997, p. 602). Typically, a learning community is arranged by having students enroll together as a cohort in several courses linked together by a common theme. The instructors of these courses then function as a team to insure that the content of one course is related to content in other courses and to help students make connections to that content. Students in the learning community also work collaboratively in small groups or teams to solve problems, study, or develop class projects and benefit by having larger blocks of time for sustained discussions and activities.

Another variation of learning communities is paired courses. Paired courses represent a learning community because students are registered as a cohort for the same two courses. In developmental education, this is typically a reading or study skills course paired with a particular content course such as English or social science. At some institutions, developmental reading is paired with developmental writing (McCabe & Day, 1998). The paired course model not only provides a learning community for students but the content course also becomes a very specific focus for application of the skills taught in another course.

Paired courses have been demonstrated to be a successful technique for enhancing the performance of developmental students. Developmental students participating in paired courses tend to show higher levels of performance and demonstrate greater satisfaction with their instruction than students participating in traditional courses (Commander, Stratton, Callahan, & Smith, 1996; Wilcox, delMas, Steward, Johnson, & Ghere, 1997).

—∾∾—

At Sandhills Community College, about 36% of developmental students are taught using learning communities, and the institution is working to increase that percentage. Learning communities at Sandhills focus on a central theme, stress integration, provide social and cultural development, and include at least one college-level course. An important feature of these learning communities is that they include extra-curricular as well as curricular activities. Those involved in learning communities report that partnerships and ongoing collaboration between students and faculty are facilitated by the integrated curriculum and extracurricular activities of the learning community.

—∾∾—

Tips for Developing Learning Communities

- Learning communities are not for everyone, in spite of the research documenting their success; some developmental students learn best in traditional courses. Informal assessment efforts should be used to determine which students are most likely to profit from learning communities before assigning them to learning communities.
- Effective learning communities require that the faculty involved in them spend a great deal of time coordinating their efforts and activities with one another. Faculty planning to participate in learning communities should allocate several extra hours each week to communication with their learning community colleagues.
- Learning communities are a labor-intensive endeavor for faculty. Where possible, release time should be assigned at the early development and implementation stage to those faculty members involved in learning communities.

- Development and implementation of effective learning communities requires training. Faculty planning to participate in learning communities should be provided with in-service workshops in learning community development as well as a variety of readings on learning communities.

- Developmental students are unlikely to know how to participate in and profit from learning communities without some training and preparation. It is important, therefore, to clearly communicate the roles and expectations of learning community participants early in the learning community experience.

- The overall effect of learning communities is strengthened by weaving advising, counseling, tutoring, and other support services into the learning community (Adams & Huneycutt, 2001). The community of learners in a set of courses is also a community of students accessing services. Services that are well integrated into the learning community are likely to have a greater impact than if they are provided in isolation from that community.

- The National Learning Communities Project based at Evergreen State College in Washington is a valuable resource for those interested in developing learning communities. Information from this project is available at http://learningcommons.evergreen.edu.

- Student interest in learning communities can sometimes be "jump started" by giving the communities interesting titles such as "Psyched on Math" (combining psychology and mathematics) or "Words and Functions in the Real World" (combining developmental mathematics and writing).

3.2: Accommodate Diversity Through Varied Instructional Methods

Although considerable research on instructional methods for developmental students has been undertaken for the past 30 years, no single method has emerged as a panacea for the many learning problems encountered by these students. The approach best supported by research to date appears to be one of using as many different teaching methods as possible in an attempt to accommodate the needs of as many different students as possible

(Boylan, Bonham, Claxton, & Bliss, 1992; McCabe, 2000; McCabe & Day, 1998; Silverman & Casazza, 1999). In case studies of exemplary university professors, Hativa, Barak, and Simhi (2001) found that while the best instructors did not use the same techniques, they all emphasized a variety of different techniques to promote student learning.

Varied teaching methods are particularly important because developmental students are among the most diverse in contemporary higher education. They are diverse in their age and ethnicity (Knopp, 1996). They are diverse in their social and economic backgrounds (Higbee & Dwinnel, 1998). They are diverse in their reasons for being unready for college-level work (Hardin, 1998). It is axiomatic, therefore, among professional developmental educators that diverse students require diverse instructional methods.

It is unfortunate that, historically, this student diversity is rarely reflected in the instructional methods used in the typical developmental classroom. More than a decade and a half ago, Richardson, Fisk, and Okun (1983) observed classroom instruction in a sample of community college developmental courses. The authors reported that the instruction they observed was dull and monotonous; it rarely required involvement or critical thinking on the part of students.

In their observations of community college instructors teaching developmental courses 17 years later, Grubb and his colleagues (1999) found that the most frequent approach was to use lectures followed by "drill and kill" (p. 181) activities requiring low level skills of memorization and recall. Breneman and Haarlow (1998) reported similar instructor behavior, particularly in developmental mathematics, in their observations of developmental classrooms. It appears to be an unfortunate fact that many developmental instructors have relied on relatively primitive teaching techniques to deliver their course material. In the process, they have rarely attempted to accommodate student diversity through diverse instructional methods. It is even more unfortunate that this appears to have been the norm over a period of almost 20 years.

Fortunately, a developing trend among the better developmental programs may be reversing this norm. In best-practice institutions developmental instructors consistently utilize a vast array of instructional practices. Instructors at best-practice institutions typically use at least three different teaching modes to present material in every class period

(CQIN/APQC, 2000). At these institutions, the provision of differing modes of instruction is built into the instructional design process. Instructors do this deliberately and with the specific intent of accommodating the diverse learners present in their developmental classrooms.

The instructional methods most often used in best-practice institutions included:

- distance learning,
- self-paced instruction,
- individualized instruction,
- peer review of student work,
- collaborative learning,
- computer-based instruction,
- mastery learning,
- small-group work, and
- other active learning techniques.

This did not mean that developmental instructors needed to abandon the lecture-discussion method, particularly if they were comfortable with it and experienced success with its use. Lectures were used quite frequently by instructors at best-practice institutions (CQIN/APQC, 2000). They were simply not the sole technique used for teaching. Other techniques such as small-group discussions, group problem solving, or the use of Classroom Assessment Techniques (Angelo & Cross, 1991) were used with regularity.

—⚬—

The approach to pedagogy at Richland College is to offer as many different options for student learning as possible. The college not only encourages different teaching methods in individual classrooms, it also makes alternative methods of taking developmental courses available to students. Some of the options available for developmental courses at Richland include computer-based learning instead of classroom instruction, small-group discussion sections, experiential learning, paired courses, weekend classes, or intensive 8-week "fast track" developmental courses. All this is supported by a commitment to professional development to help faculty learn about, implement, and monitor the outcomes of diverse instructional techniques.

———〜〜〜———

Tips for Accommodating Diversity Through Variety in Instruction

- Faculty must be provided with training in alternative forms of instruction if they are expected to use diverse instructional methods. Faculty development workshops focused on alternative teaching and learning models can be an appropriate training method. The use of study groups to implement alternative instructional approaches, share problems in implementation, and discuss solutions is also a promising technique for encouraging diversity in instruction.

- Many institutions collect information on students' learning styles in order to promote diversity in instruction. In these institutions, a learning styles inventory is administered to incoming students, usually as part of the regular assessment process. Information from these assessments is then shared with faculty who are encouraged to deliver their instruction in modes that will accommodate dominant learning styles.

- Unstructured individual study is not generally an instructional alternative from which the lowest level developmental students will profit. Developmental students who have weak study skills, poor time management skills, and low-level independent learning skills are not good candidates for independent study assignments.

- Many community colleges have experienced disappointment with intensive, short-term, or "fast track" developmental courses. Not all students have the motivation and the discipline to manage the pace in such courses. It is recommended, therefore, that some screening mechanism be used to determine which developmental students are good candidates for intensive, short-term courses rather than placing students in them randomly.

- Researchers (Canfield, 1976; Lemire, 1998) have reported some evidence that the preferred modes of learning among developmental students are visual and hands on. They learn best when they have visual representations of the concepts being discussed or when they have an opportunity to actually manipulate objects associated with these concepts. Having students view video tapes or computer graphics, use manipulatives or design Power Point presentations are often effective learning devices in developmental courses.

- The reward system for faculty should recognize the use of diverse instructional techniques if they are expected to employ such techniques. An example of this might be the submission of a teaching methods portfolio to be included as part of the salary, tenure, and promotion review process.

3.3: Use Supplemental Instruction

Supplemental Instruction or SI is probably the single most well documented intervention available for improving the academic performance of underprepared students. Blanc, DeBuhr, and Martin (1983) found that the use of Supplemental Instruction contributed to reduced attrition among undergraduate university students. Martin and Arendale (1992) reported that the use of Supplemental Instruction resulted in improved student grades in difficult freshman-level academic courses. Boylan, Bonham, Claxton, and Bliss (1992) reported that developmental programs with the highest rates of student retention regularly used SI to support students enrolled in difficult courses. Ramirez (1997) found that developmental students exposed to SI had greater long-term retention than other students. Studies by Hodges, Dochen, and Joy (2001) and Hodges and White (2001) found that the use of Supplemental Instruction improved student motivation and contributed to improved student grade point averages. A study reported by Arendale (1998) indicated that students who participated in SI consistently obtained higher course grades than students who did not participate.

Research on Supplemental Instruction was so consistently positive that, in 1981, it was certified by the U.S. Department of Education as an Exemplary Educational Program. According to Arendale (2000), it was the first research-based higher education innovation to be certified by the U.S. Department of Education and to have its dissemination funded through the National Diffusion Network under the Office of Educational Research and Improvement.

Supplemental Instruction combines the advantages of collaborative learning with an emphasis on developing study strategies associated with a particular subject area. In SI, a student who has successfully completed a particular course leads three or more out-of-class sessions per week for students currently taking the course. In these sessions, the leader integrates what must be learned with techniques for learning it. In the process, students receive continuous feedback regarding their learning, which enables them to modify their study behaviors for the course (Arendale, 2000).

A more recent version of Supplemental Instruction is Video-Based Supplemental Instruction or VSI. This technique was developed specifically for developmental students. In this model, students add the controlled review of videotapes of instructors' lectures to Supplemental Instruction sessions. This enables students to listen to lectures at their own pace, to stop the tape and ask questions, and to review vocabulary used by the instructor.

Martin and Blanc (1994) found that varsity athletes were able to obtain higher grades and to remove themselves from probation when their courses were supported by Video-Based Supplemental Instruction. Martin and Blanc (2001) also reported that the use of VSI not only improved the percent of passing grades in courses, it also reduced the percentage of student withdrawals.

Supplemental Instruction and Video-Based Supplemental Instruction have consistently been proven to enhance the performance of underprepared college students. It is, indeed, a research-based best-practice for developmental education programs.

The Supplemental Instruction leader also sits through class with students and works closely with the course instructor to identify key course concepts and learning strategies. The SI leader does not lecture on course material but, instead, provides structured study sessions for students. A major premise of SI is that the student leader integrates study skills specifically oriented to a particular course with the content of that course. As Arendale (2000) points out, Supplemental Instruction is popular with instructors because it is seen as a continuation of the learning process initiated by the instructor.

Obviously, the selection and training of Supplemental Instruction leaders is a key to effective implementation (Martin & Arendale, 1994). Supplemental Instruction leaders are students who have previously taken a course and done well in it. They are selected on the basis of instructor recommendations. They must also undergo extensive training in the concept and application of SI.

—⟋⟍⟍—

St. Louis Community College-Meramec has been sup-porting courses through Supplemental Instruction since the mid-1990s. At present, a total of 20 courses are supported through SI each term in the areas of mathematics, psychology, sociology, chemistry, and Spanish. The program is funded through a combination of institutional and grant support.

Many community colleges have difficulty with turnover in Supplemental Instruction leaders. The program at St. Louis Community College addresses this by hiring adult students who are attending college part-time as SI leaders. As a result, they have a considerable amount of continuity of SI leaders.

—⟋⟍⟍—

Tips on Using Supplemental Instruction

- Appropriate training of Supplemental Instruction leaders is one of the most important elements of successful SI programs. Supplemental Instruction should not be implemented unless the institution is willing to make a commitment to the training of SI leaders. The Center for Academic Development at the University of Missouri–Kansas City provides a variety of resources for training including manuals, training workshops, and other resource materials.

- A major construct in the use of Supplemental Instruction is that it targets difficult courses, not difficult students. Developmental mathematics is frequently one of the most difficult courses for underprepared students. Consequently, developmental mathematics courses represent a good target for Supplemental Instruction support.

- Community colleges frequently have difficulty with long-term retention of SI leaders because their best students complete their degrees in 2 years. This makes it essential that potential SI leaders be identified and recruited during their first term on campus. This can be done through the aggressive involvement of faculty in the recruitment process for SI leaders.

- Many community colleges claim to use a "modified version" of Supplemental Instruction. Sometimes these modifications involve the use of faculty or tutors as SI leaders or the substitution of laboratory sections for SI meetings. Although these modified versions of

SI may meet with some success, they are not true Supplemental Instruction programs, and they are not likely to yield all the benefits of traditional Supplemental Instruction.

- Many of the Classroom Assessment Techniques developed by Angelo and Cross (1991) are useful in promoting student comprehension during Supplemental Instruction meetings. It is helpful, therefore, to train SI leaders in the use of Classroom Assessment Techniques.
- Technology may be incorporated into Supplemental Instruction in a variety of ways. The most common way is the use of audio and videotapes of instructors' lectures as practiced in VSI. Computer graphics, Power Point slides, and a variety of other computer applications may also be used to support Supplemental Instruction.

3.4: Provide Frequent Testing Opportunities

The importance of frequent testing was documented as a component of student mastery throughout the educational literature. B.F. Skinner first reported the positive effects of frequent testing on learning in educational experiments in 1954. Carroll (1963) argued that practically all students could master material as long as they had sufficient opportunity to practice it and that testing was an important component of such practice. Bloom (1968) also recommended frequent testing as part of a plan for reducing the differences in academic performance between students with the weakest and strongest backgrounds.

It should be noted, however, that the studies on which these observations were based were done with elementary and high school students. It remained for Keller (1968) to apply the principle of frequent testing to college students in his Personalized System of Instruction. Using meta-analysis, Kulik, Kulik, and Cohen (1979) discovered that this system had a statistically significant positive impact on student grades in all courses in which it was applied.

A key component of this system was testing over each component unit of instruction. In Keller's original system, a single course might include anywhere from 12 to 20 individual unit tests (Kulik & Kulik, 1991).

Early studies of successful community college remediation by John Roueche and his colleagues (Roueche, 1968; Roueche, 1973; Rouche &

Kirk, 1974; Roueche & Wheeler, 1973) also identified frequent testing as a way to improve student mastery of the subject matter. In a study of Texas developmental education, Boylan and Saxon (1998) found that students in developmental courses emphasizing frequent testing had higher scores on a state mandated test than those in courses that did not emphasize frequent testing. In a meta-analysis of developmental instruction, Kulik and Kulik (1991) found that final examination scores for students exposed to frequent testing were higher than those of students tested less frequently. In another meta-analysis of frequent testing and mastery learning, Kulik and Kulik (1986/87) found that frequent testing contributed to higher student performance on comprehensive final examinations.

Frequent testing does not necessarily imply the exclusive use of paper and pencil or computerized testing. Any activity that requires students to demonstrate their skills and knowledge according to some standard can represent frequent testing. Consequently, the use of quizzes, verbal questioning, recitation, group and individual projects, written papers, reports, class presentations, or completion of exercises all classify as testing opportunities.

An appropriate testing opportunity requires that:

- study or preparation be an important element of that opportunity,
- topics covered be relevant to a particular concept or unit,
- the product be graded against some standard, and
- feedback be provided to students on their performance.

It stands to reason that students who lack sufficient background knowledge and skill must study and practice to develop such knowledge and skill. Feedback from frequent testing allows developmental students to monitor their own performance based on some standard and adjust their study and practice activities accordingly. Frequently, developmental students lack the discipline to engage in such study and practice on their own. Testing, therefore, serves as encouragement for study and practice and grades on tests serve as rewards for these activities.

———✄———

In a study of Texas developmental education, Boylan and Saxon (1998) found that frequent testing characterized developmental programs with high student pass rates on the state mandated TASP test. Among the institutions with the highest pass rates on the TASP test, an average of 10 tests a semester typified developmental courses. Many of the institutions with the highest pass rates required that students take individualized, computerized, or instructor designed unit tests on the textbook in order to prepare themselves for the regular classroom paper and pencil test.

—·✕✕·—

Tips for Providing Frequent Testing

- Tests do not always have to be graded in the traditional sense in order for students to receive the benefits of frequent testing. Having students' work critiqued by classmates either through class discussion or email represents a testing opportunity.

- Practice tests may be posted to the course web site in courses utilizing the World Wide Web to support instruction. It is often a good idea to encourage students to take the practice test over a particular unit before attempting the regular test over that unit.

- Many community colleges use their learning centers as sites for test administration. Instructors provide copies of their tests to the learning center, and a center staff member administers these tests to students by appointment. This enables students to take frequent tests according to their own scheduling needs without the instructor having to administer individual tests.

- The concept of "readiness tests" is often useful for developmental instruction. Readiness tests require the student to take a pretest in order to demonstrate that they have studied and mastered material well enough to have a reasonable chance of success on the regular test. A passing score on the readiness test is required in order for a student to take the regular test over a particular chapter, unit, or concept.

- The practice of beginning class sessions with a series of questions over readings or homework assignments is an example of frequent testing. It also helps encourage students to do assigned readings or complete homework assignments before class.

- Many college textbooks include review questions at the end of each unit or chapter. Students are more likely to utilize these questions for study if they are also included as part of in-class testing activities.

• It is often useful to have students make up their own questions for inclusion on unit tests. This encourages involvement in the learning process.

3.5: Use Technology with Moderation

An interesting finding from the National Study of Developmental Education (Boylan, Bonham, Claxton, & Bliss, 1992) was the identification of an inverse relationship between the amount of computer technology used in a developmental course and pass rates in that course. Instructors who reported using computers to provide the majority of classroom instruction had significantly greater failure rates than those who reported using computers only as a supplement to classroom instruction. This was true for developmental programs at both colleges and universities. In essence, where computer technology served as the only means of instruction, developmental students performed poorly.

Similar findings were reported in the CQIN/APQC (2000) benchmarking study. Developmental instructors at best-practice institutions used technology only to provide supplementary assistance, tutoring, or individual drill and practice outside of class. They did not rely on technology as a primary instructional delivery system. In the top five best-practice institutions technology was "used in a supportive role; its use was rarely mandated by the institution" (CQIN/APQC, 2000, p. 27). Furthermore, in best-practice institutions, instructors had considerable flexibility in their choice of how to utilize computers in their classes, and they also received training in the various instructional uses of computer technology (CQIN/APQC, 2000). [2]

As desktop computers and a wider variety of instructional software became available during the 1980s, there was a move by many community colleges to have a greater share of the instructional load taken over by computers. (Kulik & Kulik, 1991). In many cases, computerized instructional laboratories became the primary mode of delivery for developmental courses, particularly mathematics.

---

[2]The software programs used most frequently were Academy Systems, Learning Plus, and PLATO.

A review of the literature, however, suggested that computers were best used as a supplement rather than as a substitute for traditional classroom instruction. Both the National Study of Developmental Education (Boylan, Bonham, Claxton, & Bliss, 1992) and the CQIN/APQC study (2000) indicated that computers were most effective in developmental education when used to provide tutoring, individual review, and supplemental laboratory work. As Kulik and Kulik (1991) pointed out:

> The computer can be an infinitely patient tutor, gently correcting and guiding learners. The computer can keep perfect records of its interactions, and from these records its performance can be improved. The computer never tires; it never grows frustrated or bored; it learns from its mistakes; it is always available. (p. 33)

Consequently, computers provide an excellent source of tutoring and supplemental learning activities.

The fact remains, however, that computers also have limitations. They cannot discuss learning problems with students, they cannot make referrals to campus services, and they cannot provide social reinforcement. These are the sorts of things that developmental instructors have traditionally provided and continue to do so better than computers. The best developmental programs, therefore, recognize the limitations as well as the strengths of technology and emphasize the importance of instruction delivered by faculty.

———

Computer-based distance learning has yet to be proven effective with developmental students. Distance learning often requires independent learning skills, study discipline, time management skills, and a high degree of motivation. These characteristics are not plentiful among developmental students.

An informal literature review conducted by the National Center for Developmental Education has revealed that, as of 2000, not a single study has appeared in the literature validating the efficacy of distance learning for developmental students (Drewes, 2001). The only distance learning efforts that have shown promise are those which combine distance learning with structured, on-campus instruction.

———

Tips on Using Technology

- Most experts on technology utilization in the classroom agree with the maxim that pedagogy is more important than technology. No amount of technology will substitute for a poorly designed course. The course should be designed first, and then technology should be selected that supports this design. Advanced technological applications should not be used simply because they exist. They should only be used when they can make a meaningful contribution to student learning.

- In spite of the vast spread of technology utilization throughout American society, there are many members of our society who are still technologically illiterate. In designing a developmental course, it should not be assumed that students know how to use computers, that they are familiar with word processing programs, that they regularly access the World Wide Web, or that they have access to email. It is a good idea, therefore, to survey students' knowledge of and access to computers before designing a course on the assumption that ready access and basic knowledge are prevalent.

- One of the simplest, yet effective, ways of using technology to support instruction is to have all students in the class send an email message to the instructor. Students' email addresses can then be easily entered into an address book for notifying students of important deadlines, clarifying assignments, or sending messages to the entire class.

- It is often beneficial to use courseware for the purpose of setting up discussion groups for students taking the course. This enables them to interact with each other more frequently in a focused manner and may also contribute to building community in the course.

- A number of developmental instructors have experienced success in having students develop their own Power Point presentations to demonstrate key class concepts. This technique promotes "hands on" as well as visual learning, both of which tend to characterize the learning styles of developmental students.

- Technology is not limited to computers. Students often enjoy having the option of checking out camcorders to videotape class projects and then showing the video as an in-class presentation.

3.6: Provide Frequent and Timely Feedback

Another reason frequent testing is correlated with improved learning is that it provides feedback to students on what they have learned and what they have yet to master. This enables students to organize and guide their study and learning activities more effectively. Clear feedback on what students have failed to master, how they have failed to master it, and what they can do to improve their performance is essential for developmental students if they are to adjust their study and learning behaviors.

Learning theorists have consistently emphasized this feedback as one of the most important stimuli to learning (Bloom, 1976; Cross, 1976; Silverman & Casazza, 1999; Skinner, 1954). The feedback itself frequently serves as reinforcement for student learning. Feedback provides recognition that the instructor has seriously reviewed student work. It is an acknowledgement that the instructor takes students' efforts seriously. It can contribute to students' beliefs that the instructor truly cares about student learning.

For this feedback to be most effective, however, it must come in a timely manner. Feedback from a test or activity of a month ago is not nearly so compelling a motivational factor for students as immediate or close to immediate feedback. Neither is delayed feedback as useful to students in guiding their study activities. Feedback to developmental students should never be delayed to the point that the lessons to be learned from it are provided too late to be applicable to the next learning task.

Clearly, the best sort of feedback to provide developmental students is immediate. In fact, one of the early arguments for programmed instruction was that it provided immediate feedback to students after they had completed a test or exercise (Skinner, 1968). Similar arguments have been made for computer-assisted-instruction over the years, and this is, in fact, one of the major ways in which computer-based instruction can benefit students (Kulik, Kulik, & Schwalb, 1986).

Obviously, instructors cannot always provide immediate feedback. They should, however, attempt to give feedback on tests and assignments as soon as possible after the test has been completed or the assignment turned in by students. In this regard, computers, in-class tutors, or instructional assistants can be a valuable tool.

Feedback should also be as specific as possible. Practically everyone who has attended college can recite stories of getting major papers back with only one or two comments such as "not college level thinking" or "argument was not sufficiently developed." This sort of feedback is particularly useless to developmental students who are likely to need much more specific direction if they are to learn from instructors' comments.

Furthermore, feedback should be provided according to specific standards of performance. If a student falls short of meeting a particular standard, it is important to specify what the standard was and where the student's work placed according to that standard. Cameron and Pierce (1994), for instance, have found that general positive feedback that was not referenced to specific performance standards actually had a negative effect on student motivation.

Developmental students should be expected to meet high but achievable standards and be provided timely information on their progress toward meeting these standards. They must also be engaged in a recurring process of correction and improvement, be encouraged to take risks and learn from mistakes, and be taught how to be constructive critics of each others' work. Frequent and timely feedback from instructors and from fellow students is an essential part of this process.

———ᗰ———

The landmark work of Mina Shaughnessy (1977) revealed, among other things that developmental students frequently engage in learned patterns of error in writing. For instance, what might appear to an instructor to be random incorrect punctuation is frequently the result of punctuation rules that students have made up for themselves. It is important for students to have immediate feedback on their error patterns in order to break their habitual erroneous punctuation patterns.

A study from St. Louis Community College's Florissant Valley Campus (1995), reported considerable success in the use of instructor-designed error analysis sheets. These were completed by students immediately after having feedback on their written work. The use of these sheets to enhance students' use of immediate feedback helped improve students' sentence structure and reduce writing errors.

———ᗰ———

Tips on Providing Frequent and Timely Feedback

- Positive feedback is most effective when it is directly related to a specific task or activity. It is far more useful to say, "You did a good job of making subject and verb endings agree," than to say, "Your writing is improving."

- Self-scoring tests are useful in providing immediate feedback to developmental students as they learn particular concepts, although they are not particularly useful in judging students' general performance. Frequently, self-scoring tests can be used as a pretest to help students determine if they are ready to take a unit or chapter test.

- Immediate feedback can be provided by students as well as by teachers. Students can be given scoring sheets and asked to grade each other's work and discuss their errors. When the students cannot understand why an answer is correct, they may then go to the instructor or an instructional assistant for an explanation.

- Computers can be used in instructional laboratories to provide immediate feedback on practice problems or questions. This is a feature included in most instructional software packages, and it is one that can be quite helpful if used effectively. The effectiveness of such software is related to how closely the content of the practice questions and exercises relate to the actual content of the course in which it is used. Instructors, therefore, should review practice questions and problems in software packages very carefully to insure that there is a direct match between concepts taught in a software program and concepts emphasized in the course.

- Many institutions provide instructional assistants to work with instructors of developmental courses. A primary function of these instructional assistants is to review students' in-class work and provide immediate corrective feedback. This function is also served by laboratory assistants in instructional laboratories.

- A simple and efficient way of providing immediate feedback is asking students questions over assigned readings at the beginning of a class period and then providing feedback on the answers. This can be particularly helpful if students are given a list of potential questions that may be asked in class at the beginning of each unit or chapter. This technique also provides a useful organizer for students' study behavior.

3.7: Use Mastery Learning

Using a combination of literature reviews and observations of successful developmental programs, John Roueche and his colleagues (Roueche, 1968; Roueche & Wheeler, 1973) have identified mastery learning techniques as an important component of effective remedial instruction. Although mastery learning is not nearly as popular today as it was in the 1960s and 1970s, the evidence has consistently suggested that it is still a highly effective instructional technique for remedial courses. Research by Cross (1976) and Kulik and Kulik (1991) has strongly supported the use of mastery learning for remedial courses because of its reported capacity for improving the performance of the weakest students.

Using meta-analysis techniques, Kulik and Kulik (1986/87) found that mastery learning contributed to improved scores on examinations for all students with the greatest improvement for the weakest students. In a national study of developmental education, Boylan, Bonham, Claxton, and Bliss (1992) found that students exposed to mastery learning techniques in remedial courses were more likely to pass these courses, obtain higher grades, and be retained in the courses than students whose remedial courses were taught using more traditional techniques. A recent study of developmental courses in Texas community colleges also found that students taught using mastery learning techniques were more likely to pass a statewide achievement test in the remedial subject area than students taking remedial courses which did not feature mastery learning (Boylan & Saxon, 1998).

Most of the best-practice institutions from the CQIN/APQC study (2000) reported the regular use of some variation of mastery learning in their developmental education courses. In this study, mastery learning was frequently reported as the major form of instructional support provided by learning centers and instructional laboratories.

Mastery learning, as proposed by Bloom (1968) and Carroll (1963) appears to be particularly effective for developmental students because it allows these students to learn material and demonstrate this learning at their own pace. Mastery learning typically provides some sort of instructional laboratory where students can seek clarification of material presented in the classroom or receive help from tutors. Computer-based instruction, workbooks, and videotapes are also provided to help students learn classroom material. This allows them to put more individual time on learning tasks and, therefore, strengthen their skills outside the classroom.

All approaches to mastery learning utilize small units of instruction and frequent testing over these units. Students must be able to master the material in one unit and demonstrate this mastery through testing before progressing to the next unit. This emphasis on mastery is beneficial to students in remedial courses because it provides regular reinforcement of concepts through testing. An emphasis on mastery requires students to develop the prerequisite knowledge for success in a given course and to demonstrate this knowledge through testing.

— ᨇ —

Mathematics faculty at Barton County Community College in Great Bend, Kansas, have dramatically improved their students' performance in developmental mathematics courses through the use of mastery learning. Using a commercial software program featuring a mastery learning component, mathematics instruction is supported through instructional laboratories providing review work, self-paced instruction, and testing. The use of this program followed extensive reviews of available software by faculty and, as a result, they are very comfortable with the software program eventually selected. An interesting feature of the program is that formative and summative data on student performance is collected regularly and used to monitor the effectiveness of developmental mathematics instruction.

— ᨇ —

Tips on Using Mastery Learning

- It is often claimed that computer-based mastery learning programs will save time for instructors, and, to a degree, this is true. Prepackaged mastery learning systems are frequently a feature of the educational software programs used in college and university learning laboratories. Because of this, computer-based mastery learning can be used as a classroom supplement without the instructor having to develop, deliver, and grade unit tests. Although this saves the instructor time during the course, it requires a substantial amount of prior planning time to integrate classroom concepts and material with instructional software.

- Although self-pacing is a major advantage of mastery learning, this feature can also contribute to student procrastination, especially among developmental students with weak independent learning skills. It is important, therefore, to require that developmental students begin preparing for and taking unit tests immediately, before the volume of material to be covered overwhelms them.

- Most developmental students do not have experience with mastery learning and self-pacing. It cannot be assumed that they can enter a mastery learning system and be successful without training. Developmental students must be taught how to use mastery learning profitably before they can participate in it effectively.

- The course instructor must work closely with laboratory personnel to determine what individualized learning resources are available, how they can be accessed, and how they can best be used in support of the course if laboratories are used to support mastery learning. Laboratory personnel can also support the course better if they are fully aware of the instructor's requirements and expectations.

- A major advantage of mastery learning is that it requires students to demonstrate mastery of skills in one topic before moving on to another topic that requires these skills. It is important, therefore, that mastery-based courses be carefully sequenced to insure that each unit builds upon the skills learned in the previous unit.

- Mastery learning programs have traditionally set the criterion for mastery at an 85% correct response rate. This translates to a B+ on most grading scales. It is recommended that 85% be considered the minimum correct response rate for mastery learning tests.

3.8: Link Developmental Course Content to College-Level Requirements

Failure to insure that there is a match between the exit requirements of developmental education and the entry requirements for the college curriculum is one of the biggest mistakes a developmental program can make. The most important measure of a developmental course's impact is whether or not students who pass the course also pass the next college course in the same subject (Boylan, 1997; Boylan, Bonham, White, & George, 2000).

If there is poor linkage between developmental courses and college-level requirements, students who complete developmental education will not be successful in the college curriculum and the program is likely to be judged a failure. Such mismatches in standards may also take place within the developmental education course sequence.

In their study of Texas developmental education, Boylan et al. (1996) found that, many colleges and universities never bothered to determine whether there was a match between the exit requirements for lower level developmental courses and the entry requirements for higher level developmental courses. This remained true even in cases where large numbers of students completing lower level developmental education courses subsequently failed the next level developmental course.

This is why Roueche and Roueche (1993, 1999) have consistently argued for a seamless transition between developmental education and the college curriculum. Their studies of community college developmental education found that insuring the linkage between basic skills and college-level courses was a key component of successful programs. Similar findings were reported in a recent study of Texas developmental education: Developmental programs that insured consistency between the exit standards for developmental education and entry standards for the college curriculum had higher rates of retention than programs that did not attempt to insure such consistency (Boylan & Saxon, 1998).

Such linkage was also found to characterize best-practice institutions in the CQIN/APQC study (2000). At best-practice institutions, substantial efforts were undertaken not only to teach content but also to link thinking skills required in college-level courses to content. Among the most important of these skills were critical thinking, reflective writing, and critical reading. Researchers in developmental education have consistently found these skills to be essential for learning and mastery of the college curriculum (Chaffee, 1992; St. Clair, 1995/95; Weinstein, Dierking, Husman, Roska, & Powdrill, 1998). Chaffee, in fact, refers to critical thinking skills as the "cornerstone of developmental education" (p. 2).

In situations where faculty teach both developmental and college-level courses in the same subject, there is a built in mechanism to insure that students who complete developmental courses are ready for their next college-level course. There is no such mechanism, however, in situations where adjunct faculty are hired exclusively to teach developmental courses.

The increased use of adjunct faculty to teach developmental courses (Shults, 2000) makes it increasingly important for colleges to make every effort to insure that there is a strong link between developmental course content and college-level performance requirements.

—⚶—

The developmental studies program at Durham Technical College works closely with the Arts and Science college transfer program to insure linkage between the two programs. Syllabi from courses in the Arts and Science division are periodically reviewed by developmental faculty to insure that key concepts in Arts and Science courses are emphasized in developmental courses. Developmental reading courses typically use textbooks for Arts and Science courses as a focus for reading activities. Arts and Science faculty frequently serve as guest lecturers in developmental courses. Developmental faculty and Arts and Science faculty often team-teach the college's study skills courses for developmental students.

—⚶—

Tips for Linking Developmental Course Content to College-Level Requirements

- Faculty teaching developmental content should meet with the faculty teaching college-level courses to share and review syllabi each year. This helps to identify any areas in which there may be a mismatch between the content of developmental courses and the skills required in later courses. This also promotes confidence in developmental education among faculty outside the developmental program.

- Those who pass the highest level developmental English course and take the first college-level course in English pass at a rate of 90% according to the National Study of Developmental Education (Boylan, Bonham, Claxton, & Bliss, 1992). For those who take the highest level of developmental mathematics and then take the first college-level math course, the pass rate is 77%. If pass rates in college-level courses for those who complete the highest level developmental course are significantly lower than these rates, there is a likelihood of a mismatch between developmental and college-level content expectations.

- Those who teach developmental courses are frequently qualified to teach in college transfer programs. To the extent possible, those teaching developmental English and developmental mathematics should also teach transfer-level English and mathematics courses periodically.

- Developmental faculty at some institutions do not have the credentials to teach college-level courses. In such cases developmental instructors may still team teach the college-level course with another, appropriately credentialed faculty member. This helps to insure that they understand what preparation is required in developmental education to prepare students for college-level courses.

- Adjunct faculty should review the syllabi of the courses their students will enter upon completion of developmental education if they teach only developmental courses. Adjunct faculty should also participate in any curriculum review activities of the developmental program.

- The content of exit examinations for developmental courses should be reviewed by those instructors who teach introductory college-level courses in the same discipline. This helps insure that there is a match between the exit criteria for developmental courses and the entry criteria for college-level courses.

3.9: Share Instructional Strategies

As Grubb and associates (1999) point out, it is unfortunately true that community college personnel rarely have time to discuss teaching methods and share instructional strategies with one another. This is unfortunate because no one instructor has all the answers to the myriad problems of teaching and learning. There is much that faculty members can learn from one another by sharing experiences and problems from their courses and discussing solutions. A synergy often results when one instructor's methods are applied, refined, and shared among colleagues.

Although faculty members may claim they seldom have time to do this, the best-practice institutions identified in the CQIN/APQC (2000) study made sure that the time was available. Of the institutions completing the CQIN/APQC screening survey, 89% indicated that they had some sort of mechanisms in place to promote the development and sharing of instructional strategies at the program or discipline level. They not only promoted this sharing among instructors, many institutions also reported that they made efforts to foster collaboration between faculty members and student affairs personnel (CQIN/APQC).

Furthermore, best-practice institutions promoted this sharing on a routine basis. It was not an occasional or a random practice; it was structured into the activities of the developmental education program. Sharing of instructional strategies was a systematic part of successful developmental programs.

Best-practice institutions promoted sharing by setting aside time at faculty meetings to discuss teaching and learning issues or by forming teams of instructors to exchange teaching strategies and techniques. They encouraged sharing of syllabi and the establishment of mentoring relationships. They frequently held college-wide forums to discuss and share instructional strategies. In essence, best-practice institutions recognized that their faculty were valuable resources for each other and provided structured opportunities for such resources to be shared.

—〰—

Oakton Community College promotes sharing through brown bag lunches, departmental meetings, and workshops. It also encourages hallway conversations on teaching and learning issues and one on one meetings of faculty. In addition, the ESL program holds monthly meetings to discuss particular teaching and learning topics. An end of semester party is also held to build comraderie among the developmental education faculty. All of these activities are designed to promote the sharing of instructional strategies among faculty.

—〰—

Tips on Sharing Instructional Strategies

- Initial efforts to share instructional strategies can be undertaken on a departmental or program level by discipline. One or two meetings of discipline area faculty each semester might be devoted to the sharing of instructional strategies. It is particularly important to invite adjunct faculty to participate in these meetings.

- It is often a good idea to use short research articles on particular teaching strategies as a focus for discussion in small group meetings of faculty. These should be sent out in advance and faculty members should be advised that the article will serve as a basis for discussion at the next faculty meeting.

- Many academic departments in community colleges use email networks as a forum for discussing instructional strategies. Faculty can use these networks to describe innovative activities they use in their classes, articles on teaching strategies can be posted to the discussion site, and participating instructors can post feedback or comments on the network.

- An excellent source of information on teaching strategies is *The Teaching Professor*, a monthly newsletter featuring brief articles on particular teaching techniques appropriate for postsecondary education. Information on *The Teaching Professor*, is available from Magma Publications: (800) 433-0499 or grg@psu.edu.

- Another source of instructional strategies is *Innovation Abstracts*, published by the National Institute for Staff and Organizational Development at the University of Texas–Austin.

- Attending professional conferences is an excellent way of learning about useful or innovative instructional methods. Those who attend conferences at institutional expense should be expected to report back to their colleagues on interesting instructional strategies they have learned at the conference.

3.10: Teach Critical Thinking

Both Grubb et al. (1999) and Koski and Levin (1998) argue that an overemphasis on basic skills instruction is detrimental to developmental students. They suggest that teaching basic writing, reading, or mathematics without emphasizing application, transfer, or thinking skills not only makes remediation seem trivial to students but also fails to prepare students to be successful in later college courses.

This sentiment is echoed by Chaffee (1992) who points out that the ability to think critically–to use logical structures of reasoning, to analyze information, and to apply these in understanding concepts and solving problems–represents an essential set of skills for college success. However, as he points out, students in general and developmental students in particular are rarely taught these skills in high school or in their early college courses (Chaffee, 1992). Because of this, a lack of well-developed critical thinking skills is often a causative factor in the failure of developmental students.

Long-term studies at LaGuardia Community College have demonstrated that critical thinking instruction contributes to:

- improved student grades,
- higher course completion rates,
- enhanced intellectual maturity, and
- greater satisfaction with instruction among developmental students (Chafee, 1992, 1998).

Harris and Elsner (1997) found that teaching critical thinking resulted in improved student satisfaction with learning. St. Clair (1994/95) reported that students who were taught critical thinking in writing classes demonstrated improved research skills. Based on their review of the literature on critical thinking programs for developmental students, Koski and Levin (1998) suggested that the teaching of critical thinking enabled students to transfer problem solving and thinking skills to content area courses.

Most best-practice programs in the CQIN/APQC study (2000) emphasized critical thinking in some way. Some programs integrated critical thinking activities into reading and study strategies courses, some provided voluntary workshops on critical thinking, and some attempted to integrate critical thinking activities into the entire developmental curriculum. All of them, however, recognized the importance of critical thinking to college success and included it in one or more aspects of their services and instruction.

Although many developmental education programs provide specific courses in critical thinking, there is some evidence that this is not the most effective way to teach critical thinking to developmental students. Elder and Paul (1996), for instance, argue that because critical thinking is a developmental process it is learned most effectively when it is developed over time. Boylan, Bonham, Claxton, and Bliss (1992) have found that stand-alone critical thinking courses result in less of an impact on student grades and retention than the integration of critical thinking into all developmental courses. The research of John Chaffee (1998) suggests that the most effective way to teach critical thinking is to emphasize critical thinking concepts and methods throughout the college curriculum.

———✳———

One of the best known methods of integrating critical thinking into the curriculum is the model used by LaGuardia Community College in New York City. In this model, a series of courses emphasizing these skills are linked to the content reading, writing, and communication courses. The major critical thinking skills emphasized in these courses are: to solve challenging problems; to analyze complex issues and arrive at reasoned conclusions; to establish appropriate goals and design plans for action; to analyze complex bodies of information and make informed decisions; to communicate effectively through speaking, discussing, and writing; and to critically evaluate the logic, relevance, and validity of information.

———✳———

Tips for Teaching Critical Thinking

- There are many schools of thought as to what constitutes critical thinking and how it should be taught. It is important for developmental instructors in a particular program to agree on a definition of what they mean by critical thinking before attempting to teach it in developmental courses.
- Critical thinking is most likely to be transferred when it is integrated into all developmental courses and consistently reinforced throughout the curriculum, although stand alone critical thinking courses can be of benefit to developmental students.
- Critical thinking is best taught in a systematic manner that actually models the concept of logical structuring. It is important, therefore, to integrate critical thinking concepts and applications into a course as it is being designed.

- It is often useful to demonstrate personal models of critical thinking by having students develop their own problem solving protocols or establish their own rubrics for organizing information because developmental students frequently lack such models. These may then be discussed in class or shared with other students to determine how effective they are.

- Many students do not understand the difference between structured problems, for which there is a known correct answer, and unstructured problems, for which there is no known correct answer. It is useful, therefore, to provide illustrations of both types of problems and give examples of how the processes for solving these problems might differ.

- One aspect of critical thinking that often eludes developmental students is that there are usually many steps involved in gathering information and making decisions in solving any problem. It is important, therefore, to show students how various steps are involved in applying good problem solving skills. This can be accomplished by giving students multi-step instructions for solving a particular problem and then requiring them to demonstrate how they went through all the steps in formulating a conclusion.

3.11: Teach Learning Strategies

Many developmental students not only lack critical thinking skills but also have little understanding of the strategies required to learn new information. As Weinstein (1985) points out, developmental students are often unable to monitor their own comprehension. They do not understand when they understand and when they do not understand new material, concepts, or processes. Furthermore, even when they do realize they are not understanding, they often do not know what to do differently in order to improve comprehension (Weinstein, 1988). Young and Ley (2001) point out that teaching comprehension monitoring and self-regulating behaviors are essential tasks for developmental educators. Recognizing this, many successful developmental programs provide their students with some sort of training in learning strategies (Boylan, Bonham, Claxton, & Bliss, 1992; CQIN/APQC, 2000).

Weinstein, Dierking, Husman, Roska, and Powdrill (1998) found that students taking a learning strategies course at the University of Texas–Austin, had substantially higher retention rates, grades, and graduation rates than students who did not take the course. Commander and Valeri-Gold (2001) reported that students' self-reported awareness of their own learning increased when they were taught comprehension strategies using learning portfolios. Husman, Derryberry, and Crowson (2000) found that teaching learning skills to students enhanced their motivation and cognitive effort. McKeachie (2002) presented a variety of evidence indicating that teaching learning strategies contributed to greater student mastery and retention of subject matter.

Unlike critical thinking courses, strategic learning courses focus on specific learning strategies enabling students to monitor their comprehension, to manage a variety of learning strategies, and to evaluate the application and effectiveness of their choices. Such courses provide instruction in both the theoretical underpinnings of strategic learning and the practical application of strategic learning strategies. The emphasis is not necessarily on becoming better critical thinkers, generally, but on becoming more sophisticated in thinking about their own learning.

In order to help students engage in more strategic learning, developmental instructors need to encourage students to understand their strengths and weaknesses as learners. In the process, they must also teach students to observe and record their progress in learning and cultivate in their students a desire to know what they do not know. Once students have learned to comprehend when they understand and when they do not, developmental students must also be taught to employ alternative strategies to facilitate the learning of material they do not understand.

What has become the model strategic learning course was designed by Claire Ellen Weinstein at the University of Texas–Austin. This course emphasizes four major components as described by Weinstein, Dierking, Husman, Roska, and Powdrill (1998):

- skill, or cognitive knowledge, strategies, and study skills;
- will, or motivation and self-efficacy for learning;
- self-regulation, or time management and comprehension monitoring; and
- academic environment, or social support available and the nature of the task at hand.

Based on these main points, students learn to strategically match their selection of learning strategies to task demands and their own learning goals, to identify problems and potential problems in the application of these strategies, and to generate alternative plans based on solution-relevant factors in the context of particular learning situations.

A major benefit of strategic learning instruction is that students are able to transfer the knowledge gained to other subjects and courses. Furthermore, these benefits appear to last over time as evidenced by the fact that those who take the strategic learning course have higher rates of long-term retention than students who do not take the course (Boylan, 1999).

—⧓—

Since 1977 a strategic learning course has been taught at the University of Texas–Austin. The course, Educational Psychology 310, is a 3-credit elective offered for graded credit. Sixteen sections of this course are taught each semester by graduate students in the educational psychology doctoral program. Each of the graduate students teaching the course receives extensive training in the strategic learning model as well as in teaching techniques. The course model is highly structured with all sections having the same content, pacing, policies, testing, and assignments.

A 5-year study of the impact of EDP 310 indicated that 71% of students entering in 1990 who successfully completed the course graduated within 5 years. Only 55% of students who entered in 1990 and did not take the course graduated within 5 years (Weinstein, Dierking, Husman, Roska, & Powdrill, 1998).

—⧓—

Tips for Teaching Learning Strategies

- A major failing of many strategic learning courses is that, although they teach learning strategies, they do not teach students how to select and evaluate the appropriateness of particular learning strategies for mastering specific tasks. If students learn a strategy in a particular context, they are likely to limit their application of the strategy to that context. It is important to teach learning strategies in a variety of contexts to encourage students to apply these strategies to different situations.

- Comprehension monitoring is an essential learning strategy for developmental students. Frequently, these students not only fail to understand when they do not comprehend material, they do not know what to do differently in order to facilitate understanding. Teaching students to monitor their comprehension and to adjust their learning behaviors when they do not comprehend is an important component of learning strategies instruction.

- Knowledge of the underlying theories that make the use of learning strategies effective helps students apply them in a variety of contexts. Teaching the theory behind learning strategies is as important as teaching the strategies themselves.

- A major purpose of any learning strategies course should be to teach students to transfer these strategies to learning in other courses. It is valuable, therefore, to use real material from other courses students are taking as a focus for the transfer and application of the learning strategies.

- An important part of learning strategies is understanding and using available resources to enhance one's own learning. Such resources may include study groups, tutoring, learning assistance programs, or instructors. Teaching students how to obtain help from peers, from instructors, and from institutional services should be an important component of any course in learning strategies.

- The Learning and Study Strategies Inventory (1987), published by H & H Publishing Company and the Study Behavior Inventory (1987), published by Andragogy Associates, are both useful tools for teaching students to identify their learning strengths and weaknesses.

3.12: Use Active Learning Techniques

The APQC/CQIN (2000) study has reported that the use of active learning techniques was frequently cited by best-practice institutions as a major factor in the success of their developmental instruction. Preliminary results from the Community College Research Center's study of remediation in community colleges indicates that active learning is a key component of successful developmental education (Perin, 2001). McKeachie (2002) suggests that active learning is the most effective teaching technique available to college instructors. Tomlinson (1989) cites active learning techniques as being appropriate for developmental students because of their past failures in traditional learning environments. Wlodkowski and Ginsberg (1995) report that active learning techniques contribute to the motivation of adult students and that they are particularly useful in the teaching of nontraditional students. Stahl, Simpson, and Hayes (1992) recommend active learning as essential for "high-risk" students because it requires more involvement in their own learning. Grubb (1999) suggests that active learning techniques are most appropriate for developmental students because they foster higher order thinking than traditional instructional techniques for students who have had the fewest opportunities to develop higher order thinking and learning skills. Young and Shaw (1999) found that those college and university teachers judged by peer and student evaluations to be most effective consistently used active learning techniques in their classes. Langer (2001), reports that the use of active learning techniques helps low-achieving students improve their reading and writing skills.

The concept of active learning was originally proposed by the Brazilian educator Pablo Friere. Friere (1970) argued that traditional learning techniques tended to disenfranchise students from lower class, non-traditional, or minority backgrounds because these techniques required them to accept the "truth" of what was being taught even though their experiences may have lead them to a different "truth."

Although the original definition has been revised, redefined, interpreted, and modified in many ways, the basic concept of active learning is that students are directly involved in creating their own learning rather than being passive recipients of instruction (Friere). In active learning, students are not required to spend all of their time sitting through lectures but, instead, are required to take actions and explore knowledge for themselves.

Perin (2001), refers to methods which actively involve students as "learner centered" (p. 54). Grubb et al. (1999) refer to these methods as elements comprising "constructivist" (p.32) teaching. McKeachie (2002), notes that most active learning methods are really "peer learning."

Whatever they are called, active learning methods are characterized by the fact that they are designed to elicit students' active participation in the learning process. Such involvement is critical for developmental students because, as Grubb (1999) points out, these students have already been exposed to the typical lecture, discussion, drill and practice approaches used in high school courses and college remediation and they have not worked. Developmental students have already demonstrated their inability to learn through these methods.

Some of the active learning methods that have been utilized by participants in the CQIN/APQC study (2000) include:

- student engagement in problem solving groups,
- student design and delivery of in-class presentations on relevant course topics,
- student discussion and criticism of each others' written work,
- student journal writing reflecting classroom experiences,
- students providing coaching to each other in solving mathematics problems,
- students engaging in simulation games involving real-life experiences related to course content,
- students preparing for and leading class discussions,
- students interviewing local employers to learn about the importance of basic skills in the workforce, or
- students writing sample test questions reflecting what they consider to be the major points of classroom lectures.

These represent only a handful of the many active learning techniques available for teaching developmental students. As a glance at this list indicates, all of them involve "hands-on" activities that enable students to make personal connections to learning.

—◆—

Richland College provides several professional development opportunities for faculty to learn the best of current teaching techniques. Among these is a 3-day "Great Teaching Seminar" offered for its faculty. This seminar emphasizes active learning techniques in a variety of ways. Of particular note is the fact that participants design and implement their own format for the seminar. This demonstrates active learning principles in the very design process for the seminar. Instructors then engage in peer learning as they share and discuss their own teaching strategies with each other.

—◆—

Tips for Using Active Learning

- A simple, yet effective, way of introducing active learning is to have students determine the rules by which class discussions will be guided. In the very first session, students can be asked to identify what discussion behaviors are appropriate, how to show respect for others' points of view, how to deal with interruptions, or what the instructor's role should be in class discussions. These parameters can then be reproduced and distributed to students as a guide to classroom behavior. When this is done opportunities for students to revise these rules based on experience should also be provided.

- The instructor should not assume that students know how to operate effectively as a group when using group activities. The instructor who uses group activities should first discuss with students such things as how to develop consensus, how to set goals, how to assign tasks, or how to reach agreement on group roles. Unless this is done, it is very likely that groups of developmental students will be unable to accomplish group tasks in a timely manner.

- Some students have been so indoctrinated into passivity that it is difficult for them to become actively involved in learning. They have neither experience nor practice in active learning and they are reluctant to experiment with it. The best developmental instructors identify these students early in the course and work with them to encourage their gradual involvement in classroom learning activities.

- Active learning may be either problem centered or content centered. The former focuses on solving some problem using concepts relevant to the subject at hand. The latter focuses on teaching the subject matter. Both can have their place in active learning, but it is important for instructors not to confuse the two and to know which one they are using and why.

- It is important to provide feedback to the group as to how well they are meeting some standard when utilizing group projects in support of active learning. Standards may include arriving at an appropriate response, using an appropriate process, or working together effectively. It is also important to celebrate the success of groups who meet these standards.

- Classroom Assessment Techniques as advocated by Angelo and Cross (1991) are a very effective way of implementing active learning in the developmental education classroom.

3.13: Use Classroom Assessment Techniques

One of the major recent instructional innovations in higher education has been the development, dissemination, and implementation of Classroom Assessment Techniques (CATs), a series of active learning activities originally designed by Angelo and Cross (1991). Classroom Assessment Techniques represent what is probably one of the most successful higher education innovations in the decade of the 1990s. It is also a technique used widely by best-practice institutions in the CQIN/APQC (2000) study.

Cross (1993) argues that the use of classroom assessment helps to narrow the gap between what is being taught and what is being learned in the developmental classroom, thus increasing student mastery of the subject matter. Cross (1997) reports that the use of Classroom Assessment Techniques helps students build upon the skills learned in the classroom and, consequently, become more sophisticated learners.

Fabry, Eisenbach, Curry, and Gordon (1997) found that students exposed to Classroom Assessment Techniques reported improved understanding of course material and a more favorable attitude toward instruction. Becker and Haugen (2001) reported that the use of Classroom Assessment Techniques contributed to improved intrinsic motivation among students.

A key concept in Classroom Assessment Techniques is that teaching and learning are improved when students and instructors have feedback about how well students are learning what they are being taught. The purpose of classroom assessment, therefore, is to provide faculty and students with information and insights necessary to both guide their learning and adjust their teaching and learning behaviors (Angelo, 1991).

Classroom Assessment Techniques are a collection of short, in-class, assessment activities enabling students to identify what they have learned and faculty to use this information to adjust instruction. The most well known and widely used of the Classroom Assessment Techniques is the

"One Minute Paper" designed by Angelo and Cross (1991). The one minute paper simply requests that students write down at the end of each class period (usually on an index card) the answers to two questions: 1) what did you learn today that was most useful or meaningful, and 2) what questions do you still have at the end of today's class?

Another example is "The 'Muddiest' Point" exercise. In this technique, students are asked to use index cards to describe "What was the 'muddiest' point in this session. In other words, what was least clear to you?" (Angelo & Cross, 1991).

In either exercise, the cards are collected by the instructor who then begins the next class period by clarifying whatever major questions still exist for students. The first question in the one-minute paper enables instructors to determine if what they consider to be important from a given class session is consistent with what students have indicated as important. The second question in the one-minute paper enables instructors to identify those points that students have the greatest difficulty comprehending.

These are just two of the simplest examples of Classroom Assessment Techniques. Other Classroom Assessment Techniques enable faculty to assess student knowledge at a variety of levels in a variety of ways.

As a prelude to using Classroom Assessment Techniques, Angelo and Cross also designed the Teaching Goals Inventory which appears in *Classroom Assessment Techniques: A Handbook for College Professors*, (Angelo & Cross, 1991). This inventory provides instructors with a means of identifying their major instructional goals. The 53-item Teaching Goals Inventory also comes with a self-scoring rubric to assist instructors in prioritizing their teaching goals. This information can then be used to select appropriate questions and methods for using Classroom Assessment Techniques.

———

The United States Military Academy has instituted a version of Classroom Assessment Techniques known as the "Interim Course Feedback System." The system is based on a list of 20 open ended questions typically used in classroom assessment activities such as , "The most important thing I have learned in this course is...,""I would have an easier time learning in this class if...," or "I would improve this course by..."

The instructor selects questions from this list to be asked at different points in the term. Students are then directed to a web site for that class and required to answer these questions. Responses are collected electronically, and a separate email without student identification is then sent to the instructor recording the responses of every student in the class.

—∽∽—

Tips for Using Classroom Assessment Techniques

- Instructors using Classroom Assessment Techniques for the first time should apply them in a course they are comfortable with and know well. This insures that the effectiveness of the CATs will not be hampered by the instructor's inexperience in teaching the course.
- Instructors should never use a Classroom Assessment Technique unless they are prepared to provide feedback to students based on what is revealed through the CAT. For Classroom Assessment Techniques to work properly, it is essential that instructors "close the loop" by providing feedback to students based on their responses to CATs.
- Instructors should identify which technique is most relevant to the questions for which they want to solicit the answers when selecting Classsroom Assessment Techniques. They should not attempt to fit their questions into a particular CAT.
- The purpose of classroom assessment is to improve learning. When determining which CAT to use, it is important to ask, "How can I use the information from this technique to improve learning in my class?
- It is frequently helpful to begin using Classroom Assessment Techniques as part of a group effort. Several instructors should work together to implement CATs in their classes. This not only provides a support group for Classroom Assessment Technique utilization, it also enables instructors to share their experiences with each other in order to improve their use of CATs.

CHAPTER 4

Matching Your Own Program Against Best Practices

The inventory which follows is designed to help you compare your institution's developmental education activities to the research-based best practices described here. It is beneficial if this inventory is completed by a small group of developmental education faculty and staff. Each individual in the group should first rate each item according to their own perceptions. Once this is done, individuals should then share their ratings with the group and explain their reasons for rating each item as they have. After this, a group rating should be developed. The goal of this exercise is to reach consensus on the extent to which developmental education activities on your campus represents the best practices in the field. Once this consensus has been reached, developmental educators may then begin identifying priorities for change.

Rating Scale
1 = strongly disagree   2 = disagree   3 = agree   4 = strongly agree

---

Organization and administration

____ 1. We have a centralized developmental education program.

____ 2. We have a highly coordinated developmental education program.

____ 3. Expectations for developmental education are well-managed.

____ 4. There is collaboration between developmental education and other campus units.

____ 5. Our developmental program has a clearly defined statement of mission, goals, and objectives.

____ 6. Developmental education is an institutional priority.

____ 7. The institution provides comprehensive services in support of developmental education.

_____ 8. Grant funds are used to support innovation in developmental education.

_____ 9. Developmental education is integrated with campus outreach services in the community.

> **Organization and administration: Maximum possible score = 36**
> **High score = 27   Average score = 18   Low score = 9**

Program components

_____ 10. Assessment is mandatory for all entering students.

_____ 11. Placement in courses is mandatory based on assessment.

_____ 12. A systematic plan is in place for the evaluation of developmental education courses and services.

_____ 13. Formative evaluation is used by developmental educators to refine and improve courses and services.

_____ 14. Professional development for developmental educators is consistently supported.

_____ 15. Tutoring is provided to developmental students in all basic skills subjects.

_____ 16. Tutors working with developmental students are required to participate in training activities.

_____ 17. Developmental educators are regularly involved in their professional associations.

_____ 18. Adjunct faculty are treated as an important resource for developmental education.

_____ 19. Student performance is systematically monitored by faculty and advisors.

_____ 20. A written philosophy statement guides the provision of developmental education courses and services.

_____ 21. Classrooms and laboratories are well integrated.

Program Components: Maximum possible score = 48
High score = 36   Average score = 24   Low score = 12

Instructional practices

_____ 22. Learning communities are provided for developmental students.

_____ 23. A wide variety of different instructional methods are used in developmental courses.

_____ 24. Students are tested at least 10 times a semester in developmental courses.

_____ 25. Technology is used primarily as a supplement for instruction in developmental courses.

_____ 26. Feedback is frequently provided on a regular basis in developmental courses.

_____ 27. Mastery learning is a common characteristic of developmental courses.

_____ 28. Systematic efforts are made to link the content of developmental courses to the rest of the curriculum.

_____ 29. Instructional strategies are regularly shared among developmental instructors in some systematic way.

_____ 30. Critical thinking is taught in all developmental courses.

____ 31. Learning strategies are either embedded in developmental courses or taught as a separate course.

____ 32. All developmental instructors regularly use active learning techniques in their courses.

____ 33. All developmental instructors regularly utilize Classroom Assessment Techniques in their courses.

Instructional practice: Maximum possible score = 48
High score = 36   Average score = 24   Low score = 12

This rating scale has not yet been standardized. Although numerical ratings are provided, these are rough estimates. It should be recognized that very few developmental programs have a high rating in all of these categories. Most will fall near the average range. The purpose of this rating scale is not to compare a program to some mythical standard of perfect best practice but to identify the strengths and weaknesses of the program.

REFERENCES

Adams, S., & Huneycutt, K. (2001, July). *Learning communities in developmental education*. Presented at the Kellogg Institute for the Training and Certification of Developmental Educators, Boone, NC.

American Association for Higher Education. (1992). *Principles of good practice for assessing student learning*. Washington, DC: Author.

Angelo, T.A. (1991). Ten easy pieces: Assessing higher learning in four dimensions. In T.A. Angelo (Ed.), *New directions for teaching and learning, Number 46. Classroom research: Early lessons from success* (pp. 17-30). San Francisco, CA: Jossey-Bass.

Angelo, T.A., & Cross, K.P. (1991). *Classroom Assessment Techniques: A handbook for college teachers*. San Francisco, CA: Jossey-Bass.

Arendale, D. (1998). Increasing efficiency and effectiveness of learning for freshman college students through Supplemental Instruction. In J. Higbee & P. Dwinnel (Eds.), *Developmental education: Preparing successful college students* (pp. 185-198). Columbia, SC: National Center for the First-Year Experience and Students in Transition.

Arendale, D. (2000). *Effect of administrative placement and fidelity of implementation of the model on effectiveness of Supplemental Instruction programs*. Unpublished doctoral dissertation, University of Missouri-Kansas City.

Astin, A. (1993). *What matters in college*. San Francisco, CA: Jossey-Bass.

Becker, D.A., & Haugen, S.D. (2001, August). The effects of Classroom Assessment Techniques on accounting students. *Forum Paper*. Retrieved February 19, 2002, from the World Wide Web, http://www.accounting.rutgers.edu/raw/aaa/2001annual/sessions/ab106.pdf

Blanc, R., DeBuhr, L., & Martin, D. (1983). Breaking the attrition cycle: The effects of Supplemental Instruction on undergraduate performance and attrition. *Journal of Higher Education, 54*(1), 80-89.

Bliss, L.B., & Mueller, R.J. (1987). *Study behavior inventory*. Torrance, CA: Andragogy Associates.

Bloom, B. (1968). Learning for mastery. *Evaluation Comment, 1*(2), 2-13.

Bloom, B. (1976). *Human characteristics and school learning*. New York, NY: McGraw Hill.

Boylan, H. (1997). Criteria for program evaluation in developmental education. *Research in Developmental Education, 14*(1), 1-4.

Boylan, H. (1999). Exploring alternatives to remediation. *Journal of Developmental Education, 22*(3), 2-11.

Boylan, H., Bliss, L., & Bonham, B. (1997). Program components and their relationship to student performance. *Journal of Developmental Education, 20*(3), 2-9.

Boylan, H., Bonham, B., Abraham, A., Anderson, J., Morante, E., Ramirez, G., & Bliss, L. (1996). *An evaluation of the Texas Academic Skills Program.* Austin, TX: Texas Higher Education Coordinating Board.

Boylan, H., Bonham, B., & Bliss, L. (1994, March). *National study of developmental education: Characteristics of faculty and staff.* Paper presented at the National Association for Developmental Education Conference, Washington, DC.

Boylan, H., Bonham, B., Bliss, L., & Saxon, P. (1995). What we know about tutoring: Findings from the national study of developmental education. *Research in Developmental Education, 12*(3), 1-4.

Boylan, H., Bonham, B., Claxton, C., & Bliss, L. (1992, November). *The state of the art in developmental education: Report of a national study.* Paper presented at the First National Conference on Research in Developmental Education, Charlotte, NC.

Boylan, H., Bonham, B., White, R., & George, A. (2000). Evaluation of college reading and study strategies programs. In R. Flippo & D. Caverly (Eds.), *Handbook of college reading and study strategy research* (pp. 365-402). Mahwah, NJ: Lawrence Erlbaum & Associates.

Boylan, H., & Saxon, D.P. (1998). *An evaluation of developmental education in Texas colleges and universities.* Austin, TX: Texas Higher Education Coordinating Board.

Breneman, D.W., & Haarlow, W. (1998). *Remediation in higher education.* Washington, DC: The Thomas B. Fordham Foundation.

Brubacher, J., & Rudy, W. (1976). *Higher education in transition: A history of American colleges and universities 1636-1976.* New York, NY: Harper-Collins.

Cameron, J., & Pierce, W.D. (1994). Reinforcement, reward, and intrinsic motivation: A meta-analysis. *Review of Educational Research, 64*(3), 363-403.

Canfield, A. (1976). *The Canfield learning styles inventory technical manual.* Ann Arbor, MI: Humanics Media.

Carroll, J. (1963). A model of school learning. *Teachers College Record, 64*, 723-733.

Casazza, M., & Silverman, S. (1996). *Learning assistance and developmental education.* San Francisco, CA: Jossey-Bass.

Chaffee, J. (1992). Critical thinking skills: The cornerstone of developmental education. *Journal of Developmental Education, 15*(3), 2-8, 39.

Chaffee, J. (1998, January). *Critical thinking: The cornerstone of remedial education.* Paper presented at the Conference on Replacing Remediation in Higher Education, Stanford University, Palo Alto, CA.

College Reading and Learning Association. (undated a). *The international mentor certification program.* El Paso, TX: Tutoring and Learning Center.

College Reading and Learning Association. (undated b). *The international tutor certification program.* El Paso, TX: Tutoring and Learning Center.

Commander, N.E., Stratton, C., Callahan, C., & Smith, B. (1996). A learning assistance model for expanding academic support. *Journal of Developmental Education, 20*(2), 8-16.

Commander, N.E., & Valeri-Gold, M. (2001). The learning portfolio: A valuable tool for increasing metacognitive awareness. *The Learning Assistance Review,* 6(2), 5-18.

Continuous Quality Improvement Network (CQIN)/ American Productivity and Quality Center (APQC). (2000). *Benchmarking best practices in developmental education.* Houston, TX: American Productivity and Quality Center.

Council for the Advancement of Standards. (1986). *CAS standards and guidelines for student services/developmental programs.* College Park, MD: Consortium of Student Affairs Professional Organizations.

Cross, K.P. (1976). *Accent on learning.* San Francisco, CA: Jossey-Bass.

Cross, K.P. (1992). *Adults as learners.* San Francisco, CA: Jossey-Bass.

Cross, K. P. (1993). Closing the gaps between teaching and learning. *Journal of College Reading & Learning, 26*(1), 1-10.

Cross, K. P. (1997). *Developing professional fitness through classroom assessment and classroom research. The Cross Papers, Number 1.* Mission Viejo, CA: The League for Innovation in the Community College

Donovan, R. (1974). *National Project II: Alternatives to the revolving door.* Bronx, NY: Bronx Community College.

Drewes, S. (2001, October). *Developmental education and distance education: Findings from research and practice.* Paper presented at the conference of the College Reading and Learning Association, Spokane, WA.

Elder, L., & Paul, R. (1996). Critical thinking: A stage theory of critical thinking: Part 1. *Journal of Developmental Education, 20*(1), 34-35.

Fabry, V., Eisenbach, R., & Gordon, V.L. (1997). Thanks for asking: Classroom Assessment Techniques and students' perceptions of learning. *Journal on Excellence in College Teaching, 8*(1), 3-21.

Friere, P. (1970). *The pedagogy of the oppressed.* New York, NY: Continuum.

Garret, M.S., Porter, A., Desimone, L., Birman, B.F., & Yoon, K. (2001). What makes professional development effective? Results from a national sample of teachers. *American Educational Research Journal, 34*(4), 915-945.

Grubb, N., & Associates. (1999). *Honored but invisible: An inside look at community college teaching.* New York: Routledge.

Hardin, C. (1998). Who belongs in college: A second look. In J. Higbee & P. Dwinnel (Eds.), *Developmental education: Preparing successful college students* (pp. 15-24). Columbia, SC: National Center for the First-Year Experience and Students in Transition.

Harris, J., & Eleser, C. (1997). Developing critical thinking: Melding two imperatives. *Journal of Developmental Education, 21*(1), 12-19.

Hativa, N., Barak, R., & Simhi, E. (2001, November/December). Exemplary university professors: Knowledge and beliefs regarding effective teaching dimensions and strategies. *Journal of Higher Education, 72*(6), 700-729.

Higbee, J., & Dwinnel, P. (1998). *Developmental education: Preparing successful college students.* Columbia, SC: National Center for the First-Year Experience and Students in Transition.

Higher Education Act of 1965, Pub. L. No. 89-329, § 79 Stat. 1219 (1965).

Hodges, R., Dochen, C.W., & Joy, D. (2001). Increasing students' success when Supplemental Instruction becomes mandatory. *Journal of College Reading & Learning, 31*(2), 143-156.

Hodges, R., & White, W. (2001). Encouraging high-risk student participation in tutoring and Supplemental Instruction. *Journal of Developmental Education, 24*(3), 2-11.

Husman, J., Derryberry, P.W., & Crowson, H.M. (2000, August). *Instrumentality: An important motivational construct for education?* Paper presented at the Annual Meeting of the American Psychological Association, Washington, DC.

Keller, F. (1968). Goodbye teacher... *Journal of Applied Behavioral Analysis, 1*(2), 79-89.

Kiemig, R. (1983). *Raising academic standards: A guide to learning improvement.* Washington, DC: Association for the Study of Higher Education/Educational Resource Information Center.

Knopp, L. (1996). Remedial education: An undergraduate student profile. *American Council on Education Research Briefs, 6*(8), 1-12.

Knowles, M. (1980). *The modern practice of adult education: From pedagogy to andragogy* (2nd ed.). New York, NY: Cambridge Books.

Knowles, M. (1990). *The adult learner: A neglected species* (4th ed.). Houston, TX: Gulf.

Koski, W., & Levin, H.M. (1998). *Replacing remediation with acceleration in higher education: A preliminary report on literature review and initial interviews.* Stanford, CA: National Center for Postsecondary Improvement, Stanford University.

Kulik, C.-L., & Kulik, J. (1986/87). Mastery testing and student learning: A meta-analysis. *Journal of Educational Technology Systems, 15,* 324-345.

Kulik, J., & Kulik, C.-L. (1991). *Developmental instruction: An analysis of the research.* Boone, NC: National Center for Developmental Education.

Kulik, J., Kulik, C.-L., & Cohen, P.A. (1979). A meta-analysis of outcomes studies of Keller's Personalized System of Instruction. *American Psychologist, 34,* 307-318.

Kulik, J., Kulik, C.-L., & Schwalb, B. (1983). College programs for high risk and disadvantaged students: A meta-analysis of findings. *Review of Educational Research, 53*(3), 397-414.

Kulik, J., Kulik, C.-L., & Schwalb, B. (1986). The effectiveness of computer-based adult education: A meta-analysis. *Journal of Educational Computing Research, 2,* 235-252.

Langer, J.A. (2001). Beating the odds: Teaching middle and high school students to read and write well. *American Educational Research Journal, 38*(4), 837-880.

Lemire, D. (1998). Three learning styles models: Research and recommendations for developmental education. *The Learning Assistance Review, 3*(2), 26-40.

MacDonald, R. (1994). *The master tutor: A guidebook for more effective practice.* Williamsville, NY: The Cambridge Stratford Study Skills Institute.

Martin, D., & Arendale, D. (Eds.). (1992). *Supplemental Instruction: Improving first year student success in high risk courses.* Columbia, SC: National Resource Center for the Freshman Year Experience.

Martin, D., & Blanc, R. (1994). VSI: A pathway to mastery and persistence. In D. Martin & D. Arendale (Eds.), *New directions for teaching and learning # 60. Supplemental Instruction: Increasing achievement and retention* (pp. 83-92). San Francisco, CA: Jossey-Bass.

Martin, D., & Blanc, R. (2001). Video-based supplemental instruction (VSI). *Journal of Developmental Education, 24*(3), 12-19.

Maxwell, M. (1997). *Improving student learning skills.* San Francisco, CA: Jossey-Bass.

McCabe, R. (2000). *No one to waste: A report to public decision makers and community college leaders.* Washington, DC: Community College Press.

McCabe, R., & Day, P. (1998). *Developmental education: A twenty first century social & economic imperative.* Mission Viejo, CA: League for Innovation in the Community College.

McKeachie, W.J. (2002). *Teaching tips: Strategies, research, and theory for college and university professors.* Boston, MA: Houghton Mifflin.

Morante, E. (1989). Selecting tests and placing students. *Journal of Developmental Education, 13*(2), 2-4,6.

Muraskin, L. (1997, August). *Best practices in student support services: A study of five exemplary sites.* Washington, DC: U.S. Department of Education.

National Center for Education Statistics. (1996). *Remedial education at higher education institutions, Fall, 1995.* Washington, DC: U.S. Department of Education, Office of Educational Research and Improvement.

Neuburger, J. (1999). Executive board position paper, research and recommendations for developmental education and/or learning assistance programs in the state of New York. *Research & Teaching in Developmental Education, 16*(1), 5-21.

Noel, L., Levitz, R., Saluri, D., & Associates. (1985). *Increasing student retention: Effective programs and practices for reducing the drop out rate.* San Francisco, CA: Jossey-Bass.

Perin, D. (2001, August/September). Making remediation more learner-centered. *Community College Journal*, 53-56.

Ramirez, G. (1997). Supplemental Instruction: The long-term effect. *Journal of Developmental Education, 21*(1), 2-10.

Richardson, R. C., Jr., Fisk, E.C., & Okun, M.A. (1983). *Literacy in the open access college.* San Francisco, CA: Jossey-Bass.

Roueche, J. (1968). *Salvage, redirection, or custody?* Washington, DC: American Association of Junior Colleges.

Roueche, J. (1973). *A modest proposal: Students can learn.* San Francisco, CA: Jossey-Bass.

Roueche, J., & Baker, G. (1987). *Access & excellence: The open door college.* Alexandria, VA: The Community College Press.

Roueche, J., & Kirk, R. (1974). *Catching up: Remedial education.* San Francisco, CA: Jossey-Bass.

Roueche, J., & Roueche, S. (1993). *Between a rock and a hard place: The at-risk student in the open door college.* Washington, DC: Community College Press.

Roueche, J., & Roueche, S. (1999). *High stakes, high performance: Making remedial education work*. Washington, DC: American Association of Community Colleges.

Roueche, J., & Snow, G. (1977). *Overcoming learning problems*. San Francisco, CA: Jossey-Bass.

Roueche, J., & Wheeler, C. (1973, Summer). Instructional procedures for the disadvantaged. *Improving College and University Teaching, 21,* 222-225.

Russell, A. B. (1997). *Statewide college admissions, student preparation, and remediation: Policies and programs*. Denver, CO: State Higher Education Executive Officers.

Shaughnessy, M. P. (1977). *Errors and expectations: A guide for the teachers of basic writing*. New York, NY: Oxford Press.

Shults, C. (2000). *Institutional policies and practices in remedial education: A national study of community colleges*. Washington, DC: American Association of Community Colleges.

Silverman, S., & Casazza, M. (1999). *Learning and development: Making connections to enhance teaching*. San Francisco, CA: Jossey-Bass.

Skinner, B.F. (1954). The science of learning and the art of teaching. *Harvard Educational Review, 24*(3) 86-97.

Skinner, B.F. (1968). *The technology of teaching*. New York, NY: Appleton-Century-Crofts.

Stahl, N., Simpson, M., & Hayes, C. (1992). Ten recommendations from research for teaching high-risk students. *Journal of Developmental Education, 16*(1), 2-10.

Stake, R. (1967). The countenance of educational evaluation. *Teachers College Record, 68,* 523-540.

St. Clair, L. (1994/95). Teaching students to think using library research and writing assignments to develop critical thinking. *Journal of College Reading & Learning, 26*(2), 65-74.

Stratton, C. (1998). Transitions in developmental education: Interviews with Hunter Boylan and David Arendale. In J. Higbee & P. Dwinnel (Eds.), *Developmental education: Preparing successful college students* (pp. 25-36). Columbia, SC: National Center for the First-Year Experience and Students in Transition.

Thayer, S. (Ed.). (1995). *NADE self-evaluation guides*. Clearwater, FL: H & H Publishing.

Tinto, V. (1997). Classrooms as communities: Exploring the educational character of student persistence. *Journal of Higher Education, 68*(6), 599-623.

Tinto, V. (1998, January). *Learning communities and the reconstruction of remedial education in higher education.* Paper presented at the conference on replacing remediation in higher education, Stanford University, Palo Alto, CA.

Tomlinson, L.M. (1989). *Postsecondary developmental education programs* (ASHE/ERIC Research Report # 3). Washington, DC: Association for the Study of Higher Education.

Weinstein, C.E. (1985). Comprehension monitoring: The neglected learning strategy. *Journal of Developmental Education, 9*(1), 6-9, 28-29.

Weinstein, C.E. (1988). Executive control process in learning: Why knowing how to learn is not enough. *Journal of College Reading & Learning, 21*, 48-56.

Weinstein, C.E., Dierking, D, Husman, J., Roska, L., & Powdrill, L. (1998). The impact of a course on strategic learning on long-term retention of college students. In J. Higbee & P. Dwinnel (Eds.), *Developmental education: Preparing successful college students* (pp. 85-96). Columbia, SC: National Center for the First-Year Experience and Students in Transition.

Weinstein, C.E., & Schulte, A.C. (1987). *Learning and study strategies inventory (LASSI).* Cleawater, FL: H & H Publishing Company.

Wilcox, K.J., delMas, R.C., Stewart, B., Johnson, A.B., & Ghere, D. (1997). The package course experience and developmental education. *Journal of Developmental Education, 20*(3), 18-26.

Wlodkowski, R., & Ginsberg, M.B. (1995). *Diversity & motivation: Culturally responsive teaching.* San Francisco, CA: Jossey-Bass.

Workforce Investment Act of 1988, Pub. L. No. 105-220, § 112 Stat. 936 (1988).

Young, D.B., & Ley, K. (2001). Developmental students don't know that they don't know: Bridging the gap. *Journal of College Reading & Learning, 31*(2), 171-178.

Young, S., & Shaw, D.G. (1999). Profiles of effective college and university teachers. *Journal of Higher Education, 70*(6), 670-686.

APPENDIX

Topical Insights and Case Studies

Many of the best practices described in this book were identified through the national benchmarking study of developmental education sponsored by the Continuous Quality Improvement Network (CQIN) and conducted by the American Productivity and Quality Center (APQC). This study both verified much of what we already knew from research in the field and broke new ground by validating practices that, heretofore, had little research support.

The CQIN/APQC (2000) benchmarking study methodology involved both survey and case study analysis to identify "best-practice" partners. Survey information was originally used to identify these partners. The original survey was later followed by a 25-item questionnaire that was used to gather additional information, guide the format for on-site campus visits, and contribute to the analysis of data.

The American Productivity and Quality Center developed the questionnaire in collaboration with the National Center for Developmental Education and the CQIN partners. The questionnaire included the following items.

CQIN/APQC Benchmarking Survey Questions

1. Please describe the evolution of your institution's developmental education program and the key stakeholders involved in its creation and implementation.
2. A. Please describe the structure of your developmental education program, including how it receives funding, its placement within the organization's administrative structure, and any collaborative approaches/relationships with internal and external organizations.
    B. How was the present structure/approach selected for your DE program?
    C. What strategies and approaches taken by your DE program have been unsuccessful? How did you/will you modify these practices?

3. Describe how you integrate the various functions of your institution's DE program.

4. How is the developmental education program included in the institution's overall strategic planning process?

5. How does the institution plan for improvements to your developmental education strategy? What steps do you take to ensure input from your various stakeholders (e.g., faculty, students, alumni, and employers)?

6. Please describe the mechanisms and processes used to arrive at consensus on exit standards for your developmental education program.

7. A. What role does technology play in the overall structure of your developmental education program?

   B. What evidence do you have that applications of technology are effective in your DE program?

8. A. Describe the faculty development opportunities available to your DE faculty.

   B. Describe the resources available for professional development for your DE faculty (e.g., professional memberships and conferences). What activities in this area have been the most successful, and why? What methods are used to ensure that effective training and faculty development are deployed across all DE program elements?

   C. Do faculty development programs differ for adjunct DE faculty? If so, please explain how.

9. How does your developmental education program use release time or reassigned time (e.g., for curriculum development, program development, faculty development)?

10. Describe the curriculum development process for your DE program and how this process is supported by the institution (e.g., through faculty release time, curricular design assistance, and technology support).

11. What aspects of your developmental education curriculum contribute most to your program's success?

12. Does your institution outsource (i.e., contract with an external vendor or provider) any of its developmental education instruction? If so, please describe what is outsourced and why. Does your institution have any future plans for outsourcing instruction?

13. A. Please describe the mechanisms in place for developing teaching strategies among developmental education faculty.

   B. How are teaching strategies communicated/shared across DE departments?

14. What pedagogical approaches or methodologies have you found work best with developmental education students? Please explain.

15. Do you collect data on faculty satisfaction with your DE program? Is it collected from dedicated DE faculty only or from faculty members who also teach college-level courses? What methods are you using to collect this data? What have the results been? Please explain.

16. How does your institution asses learner skills and abilities? How are students placed in developmental education courses? Please describe the process used and its strengths and weaknesses.

17. A. Describe all of the support services (academic and personal intervention) provided to students in your DE program.

   B. How are support services organized and/or integrated with the DE program? How are they staffed and funded?

   C. Please describe the support functions or services that have contributed the most to the success of your institution's developmental education students. Which functions or services have been least helpful?

18. How is student performance monitored in your DE program? How is student performance tied to your intervention strategy?

19. Do you collect data on student satisfaction with your DE program? If so, what methods are used to collect this data? What have the results been? Please explain.

20. A. What data are your institution tracking from your developmental education program at both the student and the program levels? Do you track students beyond your own institution (e.g., into transfer colleges or work)?

   B. What methods are you using to track that data, and how did you decide on the measures used? Please explain.

21. How does your institution use the results of your DE program-level evaluation?

22. Is there a systematic evaluation of learner and instructional support services for your developmental education program? If so, please describe this evaluation.

23. A. How does your institution compile and evaluate the qualitative and quantitative data collected from learners, faculty members, etc. on your developmental education program? Who is responsible for this process? Describe your methodology.

    B. How is this information disseminated to key stakeholders? How is this feedback used (i.e., for performance improvement)?

24. If you had to do it over again, what would you do differently when developing the evaluation system for your developmental education program?

In-depth responses to these questions were collected from each best-practice partner in the preparation process of the study.

The results from survey questionnaires and site visits are the property of the Continuous Quality Improvement Network and the partners who funded this study. Information regarding access to raw data from surveys and site visitations may be obtained through the CQIN web site:

http://www.cqin.org/publications/index.asp

The CQIN/APQC (2000) benchmarking study was sponsored by the following organizations:

- Albuquerque Technical Vocational Institute
- Anne Arundel Community College
- Cincinnati State Technical and Community College
- Contra Costa Community College District
- Datatel, Incorporated
- Diablo Valley College
- Howard Community College
- Jackson Community College
- Metropolitan Community College
- Mount San Antonio College
- Northcentral Technical College
- Northwest Vista College
- Richland College
- Terra Community College

The study would not have been possible without the support of these institutions.

SUBJECT INDEX